Bikepacking Mongolia

Aktash
Акташ
Kosh-Agach
Кош-Агач
Kyzyl-Khaya
Кызыл-Хая
Тэс
Ulaangom
Улаангом
Erzin
Эрзин
Хатгал
Murun
Мөрөн
Sükhbaatar
Сүхбаатар
Khyagt
Кяхта
Darkhan
Дархан
Erdenet
Эрдэнэт
Zuunkharaa
Зүүнхараа
Khan Khen
Хан хэнти
Batsumber
Батсумбэр
Ulaanbaatar
Улаанбаатар
Altai Tavan
Bogd
National Park
Ölgii
Өлгий
Tolbo
Толбо
Khovd
Ховд
Urdgol
Урдгол
Songino
Сонгино
Telmen
Тэлмэн
Tosontsengel
Khujirt
Хужирт
Khorgo
Хорго
Aldar
Алдар
Uliastai
Улиастай
Tsetserleg
Цэцэрлэг
Lun
Лун
Kharkhorin
Хархорин
Mongolia
Jargalant
Жаргалант
Ulaantolgoi
Улаантолгой
Darvi
Bayan-Uul
Баян-Уул
Bayanbulag
Баянбулаг
Altai
Алтай
Burenkhairkhan
Бүрэнхайрхан
Khukh-Uzuur
Хөх-Үзүүр
Bayankhongor
Баянхонгор
Arvaikheer
Арвайхээр
Choir
Чойр
Mandalgovi
Мандалговь

Bikepacking Mongolia

An Epic Adventure

John VanOstenbridge

Printed in the United States of America

First Printing, 2026

ISBN-13 (Hardcover): 979-8-9950831-0-8
ISBN-13 (Trade Paperback): 979-8-9950831-1-5
ISBN-13 (eBook): 979-8-9950831-2-2

Airag Books
Nashville, Tennessee
airagbooks1@gmail.com

Dedication

This book is dedicated to my wife Val. I love you more than words can express and am thankful every day to have you in my life.

To Stephen and Carly, our two kids, and constant source of pride, joy, and love.

Thank you, Val, Carly, Tina, and John, for your proofreading and valuable editing advice.

Thank you, Jon, for being such an outstanding adventure travel buddy.

Preface

I am (or more accurately *was* now that I'm retired) a pediatrician.

For thirty years I had the honor and privilege of providing healthcare to children. Every day was full of happy kids telling exciting stories about their last soccer goal, birthday party, or new puppy. I was grateful to have parents trust my medical advice for the most important person in the world to them - their child. I appreciated the highly skilled professionals in the office, many of whom had been with me for over twenty years. I could not ask for a more competent or dedicated group of people. I have always thought that I was truly lucky to love my work and my work family.

I am thankful to have a wife who is amazing in so many ways, with an awesome sense of adventure. I have lost count of how many treks Val and I have made through jungles, canyons, and mountains. We even went SCUBA diving on the morning of our wedding day. After our two kids were born, we continued our travels as a family. They had their own passports while still in elementary school. We had many family discussions about where our next adventure would be.

As time went by, and life happened, I realized we had a bit of a dilemma. We had an adventurous family who loved to travel, but we both had busy, time-consuming careers that became more demanding with each passing year. Unfortunately, neither of us could be away from our work for more than a week at a time, which placed limits on our wanderlust. Whenever I had time to stop and eat lunch, I would find myself looking out the office window thinking it looked like a nice day for a long hike, challenging bike ride, or some other kind of outdoor fun. This lasted for a few minutes until it was time to take care of the next patient, lab result, or phone call. As much as we both loved our jobs, we also loved vacations. My pediatrician partner and I covered for each other whenever one of us was out of the office, but we were the only pediatricians in each office. Since it was just the two of us, we were essentially solo practitioners and could never take more than just a few days off at a time. While I accepted this as normal, there was always a yearning for a larger adventure.

It is said "all good things must come to an end" and so it is with careers. Val and I both retired in the summer of 2021 and moved to an area in Tennessee with hiking, biking, and kayaking nearby. I was perfectly satisfied with my new retirement life. I played with my new toys, a mountain bike and kayak, which provided a sense of freedom I had not known before. There were thoughts about what else retired guys do, like hike the Appalachian Trail and other crazy ideas. I had to sort out what was reasonable and what was simply unrealistic.

The book begins at this point. I was presented with a bizarre idea which initially seemed unrealistic but then became a curiosity. This was an opportunity to experience the adventure I had been seeking. The decision to bike across Mongolia with a guy I barely knew required quite a lot of thought. Val and I had many discussions, weighing the pros and cons of such an idiotic plan. Ultimately, we decided that adventure was calling me. I was about to do something completely crazy!

Introduction

This book did not begin as a book. The book simply started as research notes to myself.

The first portion of the book gives background information on how this trip began. What started as an idea to bike across Mongolia developed into a research project several months long. This part of the book contains the information required to plan a trip like this. Questions like "What's a Tugrik?" are explained here.

The key to success was to carefully plan and work out the logistical problems before arriving in Mongolia. I had a long list of questions without readily available answers: how to get there, obtain cash, find places to stay, get food, buy bikes, communicate home, manage the language, navigate immigration protocols, obtain equipment, prepare for weather, choose clothing, and on, and on, and on... I could find no books written about a trip like this, so countless hours of online research resulted in many pages of notes. I imagined myself being there, encountering issues, and working out solutions. While it was impossible to plan for every possible situation, I tried to prepare as well as I could. Although specific to Mongolia, much of this book can apply to many different foreign travel or distance biking adventures.

The second part of this book is based on daily journals I kept during the trip. Each day was a mini adventure by itself. Most people, including myself, do not know much about Mongolia. I only knew of it as a different, mysterious kind of place. I learned an enormous amount about a country that was unfamiliar to me and learned a few things about myself as well. In hindsight, I can truly say this was the adventure of a lifetime.

PART ONE

From Crazy Idea to Curiosity

DECEMBER 2022: WHAT?!

My wife Val and I were on vacation with our good friends Jeff and Christina. We had recently moved to Tennessee and met them at a martini party. Chris trained in California as a gourmet chef and has a cooking show on YouTube, "Thyme Saver Kitchen." I highly recommend checking out her videos, not just since she is a friend, but also because her recipes are easy to make and taste great. Although I'm not a cook, even I can do them.

In my first conversation with Jeff, I found out he enjoyed kayaking. I asked where he liked to paddle, and he said he recently finished the Mississippi River. I asked where on the Mississippi, and he said, "The whole thing." Astonished, I asked, "Do you mean you went from that lake in Wisconsin (Lake Itasca, Minnesota) to the Gulf of Mexico?" He replied, "Yep!" and told me he did it with his cousin Jon. I thought, "Wow, that's pretty beast! What an epic adventure!" Since then, Jeff and Jon have paddled the entire Tennessee River and plan to do the Ohio River next. Why two such accomplished people like Jeff and Chris would want to hang out with us has always been a mystery.

One evening during our vacation together, while we were all in a condo overlooking the sugar white sands of Pensacola Beach and the turquoise blue waters of the Gulf of Mexico, Jeff received a text message from his cousin Jon. Jeff looked at the text with a curious face. This caught our attention, not knowing if he had just received good news or bad news. He then turned to me and said, "Jon wants to know if you would be interested in biking across Mongolia with him." I looked at the startled faces of Jeff, Chris, and Val. Now that I think about it, I guess I had the same startled look. This seemed like a bizarre question. I don't remember my immediate response, but I'm sure it was a well thought out, cogent, intelligent reply - something along the lines of "What?!"

I didn't really know Jon and was surprised he would ask about something like this. I had only met him once, just after publishing his book "Paddling the Mississippi, One Story at a Time" about the trip he had done with Jeff. The only thing I knew about Jon was that he was an adventurous kind of guy, having climbed the highest mountain peaks in North, Central and South America, hiked the 2,600-mile Pacific Crest Trail, biked across Ireland, as well as numerous other crazy things. He seemed to like very remote locations like Tibet, Suriname, French Guyana, and many other places I could not even find on a map.

My total knowledge about Mongolia was that it sits between Russia and China, and the capital is Ulan Bator. In my first online search I found a lot more "a's" in Ulaanbaatar, which is the preferred spelling. Clearly, I had a lot to learn. Fortunately, Jon had already done a great deal of the pre-planning. He had been thinking about this trip for quite a long time. The idea first came up about ten years ago, when he and his son discussed taking motorcycles across Mongolia. Unfortunately, the realities of life got in the way. Having a job tends to take up a lot of your free time. The idea came up again about two years ago, but with bicycles instead of motorcycles. His son, now an airline pilot, still could not take two months off from work. Jon asked his mountain climbing buddies and other adventure pals, but no one was interested. Likely out of desperation, and finding no one else foolish enough to agree, he thought to ask me. He knew I enjoyed biking and outdoor fun and, being newly retired, I had the time.

Jon had already mapped out two possible routes with daily itineraries marked by time and distance. There were monasteries and other sights along the way that we could visit. The prize at the end was to make it to the town of Ulgii (also spelled Olgii and Olgiy) in western Mongolia by September 30th to see the Golden Eagle Festival. This annual event showcases the talents of trainers and their eagles, which are taught to hunt small prey and return it to their master. Hunting with eagles dates back at least as far as the 12th century. Some families have been training eagles for generations. Mongolia is a tough, rural country that demands self-reliance to survive. The nomadic lifestyle has existed for hundreds of years. For much of the country, it is likely the only way to survive.

The decision to undertake a trip like this obviously required considerable thought. This trip would take two months to complete, traveling on the other side of the planet without the aid of a local tour guide. The planned route is extremely remote and, if we encounter problems, help may not be available. The weather can be brutal, especially in the mountains. Food and water sources are not guaranteed. Communications are difficult at best, with a language completely unknown to me and many areas with limited or non-existent internet access. There will be large stretches of time where I am unable to contact my wife. Half a world away, she will have no idea about our health and safety. We will be traveling on unmarked roads, many being dirt roads, without the luxury of street signs. Even if there are signs, they are written in the Cyrillic alphabet, which does not help much. There is a very real possibility of getting hopelessly lost. I have traveled to some rural areas, but nothing like this.

Fortunately, Jon has much more experience traveling in remote parts of the world. His confidence and detailed planning were reassuring. Video calls and emails with Jon were frequent in the month it took for Val and me to do the online searches required to decide if I should go. It was difficult to weigh the risk of danger against the reward of adventure. Ultimately, we decided the trip was possible.

Val and I have always enjoyed trips 'off the beaten path' traveling through the jungles of Belize, trekking around in Iceland, or taking remote SCUBA trips. I think my sense of adventure had been suppressed a bit after 30 years as a pediatrician with numerous responsibilities and obligations. I was in need of a big adventure. Thus began the arduous task of doing the "real" research.

There have been times when I agreed to do things and, as the time approached, I would wonder why on earth I ever agreed to do it. Things that 'seemed like a good idea at the time' usually involve some degree of risk. Biking across Mongolia certainly had its share of risk. This trip was going to be a huge leap of faith.

PLANNING

> *"If you fail to plan, you plan to fail"*
> *—Ben Franklin*

I could not find any information about people who had taken a trip like this. We would be just two guys, completely on our own, planning to ride bicycles over a thousand miles. The usual Mongolian adventure is taking a motorcoach tour organized through a travel agency. Some have mountain bike options with an escort van, stopping at nice hotels each night. This was not the kind of trip we were planning. I was hoping to learn from other people's experiences but, since that wasn't possible, we had to research everything ourselves.

The first thing I did was to go to our small-town public library and check out everything I could find about Mongolia. Fortunately, both books were available! Even though the books were written for children, they were still helpful. Most of what I read was a brief history of Mongolia, beginning with Chinggis (Genghis) Khaan who lived 1162-1227. Chinggis Khaan is still an extremely controversial figure to this day. He is credited with essentially building the great Mongol Empire, the largest empire to ever exist, which stretched from the Sea of Japan to present day Eastern Europe. This was about five times larger than the Roman Empire. The downside, of course, is that he and his armies killed up to 40 million people by some estimates. Being both brilliant and ruthless, his name lives on. The international airport in Ulaanbaatar is named after Chinggis Khaan, along with several national monuments, streets, gardens and parks.

Mongolia is the most sparsely populated country in the world, with an average population density of 2.2 people per square kilometer, compared to the US at 34.8 people per square kilometer. Mongolia has a land mass 2.3 times larger than Texas with a total population of 3.4 million people, per 2022 data. As a comparison, the Houston metropolitan area alone has a population of 6.8 million. Considering that half of the entire country's population lives in the capital city of Ulaanbaatar, it is extremely remote outside of the city. For this trip, self-reliance was going to be crucial.

The next logical step was to search the internet. Many details were handled by online searches. We booked plane tickets, hotels, and ger camps, bought equipment and obtained a great deal of information just by looking at a computer screen. I must give Jon credit for his communication skills. Countless texts, emails and video calls allowed us to constantly share ideas and information. Both of us had individual areas to research but most things were a classic team effort. We agreed on important items like meeting at the airport in Seoul while still allowing for individual preferences such as food. It was also essential to discuss concerns like getting lost, then creating solutions. Jon made a two-volume binder of satellite imagery for the entire route, which was a valuable resource.

YouTube has several good videos ranging from vacation videos to more educational ones. Val and I enjoyed watching them together, sometimes with a bowl of popcorn. We were both wondering about the people, customs and scenery that Jon and I might encounter. Initially it felt like going to the moon but exploring Mongolia from the comfort of our living room definitely helped to reduce the anxiety of the unknown. Although I could not find anything like the trip we were planning, I felt like I learned something from each video we watched. Most people began in Ulaanbaatar, just as we planned, so seeing the city gave us a good idea of what to expect. One video featured a group of Mongolian throat singers who produced an oddly musical sound using guttural vibrations in the throat. Apparently, this is practiced by Buddhist monks in Tibet and Mongolia. Another video taught me about something not to try - a man walked across the Gobi Desert pulling a cart with supplies. He nearly died from dehydration and malnutrition. It was just another reminder that food and water were important! Val also found a great YouTube video on how to speak some essential words and phrases in Mongolian. I wrote these down phonetically and hoped it would make sense should I need to speak it.

Facebook, to me, was an unlikely source of information. Val found groups about traveling in Mongolia. Reading other people's experiences allowed us to gain insight into the people and places we were about to encounter. Being able to post questions was also extremely helpful. There were many people who gave great answers and new ideas to consider.

Nine months of research before our trip resulted in many pages of detailed notes. The following is a very brief summary of the essential information needed to complete this adventure, and provides the reader with a better understanding of events to come:

OLLY

I was introduced to Olly through Jon and only knew him as the person in Mongolia on the other end of emails. Jon had looked up travel companies in Ulaanbaatar and found Olly at Goyo Travel. Olly is fluent in English and is the one who would answer our many questions. Even though we did not actually book one of their travel packages, Olly was extremely helpful to us. Olly found places for us to stay in Ulaanbaatar for both the beginning and end of our trip, along with some ger camps for the first few nights after we left the city. He was also able to arrange plane tickets from Ulgii back to Ulaanbaatar after the Eagle Festival. This was especially helpful since there are only a few flights a week and tickets were in high demand for those leaving the festival. We did pay Olly a nominal commission for his work, but I know he was not doing any of this for the money. I give Olly a lot of credit for helping us get started, and I greatly appreciate his kindness and patience.

ROUTE

Jon had two possible routes picked out, based on the road maps he could find. There was the "northern" route, which was very scenic but much more mountainous, and the "monastery" route which, while still mountainous and a longer distance, avoided some of the higher peaks. This route allowed us to visit several historic Buddhist monasteries. After discussing our options, we decided the monastery route was the more reasonable choice. This would take us south of the highest peaks in the Khangai Mountains and north of the Gobi Desert.

One of my major concerns was the possibility of getting lost. The thought of being stranded in the extremely remote countryside, with only the food and water we happened to have in our packs, was distressing. If we were lucky enough to see another person, we would not be able to communicate as we did not speak the language. Getting lost was not an option. To alleviate both of our concerns, Jon meticulously mapped out the entire route in a two-volume binder using satellite imagery of every road, village, and intersection. Key features like gas stations, hotels, and markets were labelled. Gas stations prove there are motorized vehicles, which means something along the lines of civilization as we know it. Hotels are always welcome, since a hot shower and warm bed is much better than another night in a tent. Markets, of course, are essential. We planned to stock up on food every chance we had.

PASSPORT

Obviously, a passport is required and must be valid for at least six months after the date of arrival. It is worth looking into this early as a new passport can take months to process.

I recommend having a Global Entry card. This allows you to quickly go through US Customs when returning from out of the country.

There are automated kiosks set up where you can present your card, answer a few questions, and go on your way. Another perk is that it gives you TSA PreCheck. Avoiding those long lines at TSA screening points is well worth the application fee. The instructions on how to obtain one are outlined on the US Customs and Border Protection website (cbp.gov.)

I think it is also good practice to make copies of your passport and Global Entry card to carry with you in case either one is lost or stolen.

VISAS AND REGISTRATION

Mongolian visa requirements will vary by the country of one's nationality. Two very useful websites were immigration.gov.mn and mongolian embassy.us.

Citizens of the US visiting for 30 days or less do not need to register with the Mongolian Immigration Office. Because policy can change, it is important to check the current protocols at the time of your visit.

Visitors from the US staying 30-90 days need to register with the Mongolia Immigration Office in Ulaanbaatar within seven days of arrival. The easiest way to do this was online at immigration.gov.mn. If traveling with an organized tour group, these details will most likely be taken care of ahead of time by the tour company. The helpful folks at Goyo Travel took care of this for us, and the entire process took less than two minutes.

For visits longer than 90 days a visa is required, and information can be obtained through the immigration office website.

The US State Department has the Smart Traveler Enrollment Program (STEP) which is a free service to register your trip with the nearest US embassy or consulate office. The purpose is to assist if there is an emergency during the trip, an emergency at home, civil unrest, or a natural disaster. I registered with the STEP program thinking it would be helpful if needed. Further information is on the website step.state.gov.

CURRENCY

Mongolia uses the Tugrik (also spelled Togrog) and is abbreviated MNT. The exchange rate during our trip was roughly 3,450 MNT to one US Dollar. Initially there was a bit of "sticker shock" when I saw that each of our bikes cost well over two million Tugrik. It was a big relief after doing the math and finding out that one million Tugrik is less than $300.

Ulaanbaatar is loaded with banks and ATMs, and we were easily able to get cash when needed. Even the smaller towns had banks and ATMs, but they can be sporadic in the more rural areas. ATMs in Mongolia work exactly the same way as in the US, by inserting your bank ATM/debit card and PIN number to begin. The first screen allows a choice of the preferred language, and subsequent screens carry out the transaction.

Credit Cards are easy to use in Ulaanbaatar and most other towns but might not be accepted in the more rural areas. I brought two credit cards, along with a debit card, in case one was declined. There was only one instance where both credit cards were declined, and the debit card saved the day.

When given the choice of being charged in USD or local currency, I always prefer to choose local currency. Currency exchange rates vary constantly, and local businesses may "round up" and charge more than the current rate. If purchasing items in the local currency, the credit card company will use the accurate exchange rate for that transaction.

One last consideration is to use credit cards that do not charge foreign transaction fees. Those fees are not much, but they can add up if the credit card is used often.

FLIGHTS

Trying to arrange flights and lodging is something like a question on a college entrance exam. If a flight leaving San Francisco at 11:40 p.m. on Monday going to Seoul takes 13 hours, crosses 9 time zones and the International Date Line, when do you arrive? (Answer: 4:20 a.m. on Wednesday.) What is really bizarre is that a flight leaving Seoul at 5:40 p.m. on Wednesday arrives in Dallas at 4:35 p.m. on Wednesday, so you arrive one hour before you leave.

A helpful item I highly recommend is a luggage tracker. I used a Samsung Galaxy SmartTag and paired it to my Samsung Android phone. I secured the SmartTag inside my checked backpack to always know where my all-important pack was. I had peace of mind knowing that my backpack was indeed on the plane.

For those who have Apple phones, the Apple AirTag is a great choice. I have not personally used the Apple AirTag, but my daughter shipped several boxes to Germany for her work and was able to track them from her location in Miami.

Similar to the idea of luggage trackers are people trackers. Val and I downloaded the Life360 app on both our phones a few years ago. It comes in handy when I am out hiking or mountain biking. We were pleased to discover Life360 works worldwide. There were times during phone calls when I would describe to Val where I was, and she could send me detailed screenshots of my location. Life360 has both basic and satellite imagery maps, labeled with names of key buildings or streets. This gave us peace of mind knowing that if we needed help, at least she would have some idea of where we were.

SEOUL INCHEON INTERNATIONAL AIRPORT

Jon and I were coming from different places and decided to meet at the airport in Seoul. The Seoul Incheon International Airport is large and modern with adequate signage in English. I found it very easy to get around. The fourth floor has a wide variety of restaurants with both Asian and Western cuisines. On the lowest level there are storage lockers and a spa with showers and sleep rooms that can be rented for a reasonable price.

CHINGGIS KHAAN INTERNATIONAL AIRPORT

Known as the "new" airport, the Chinggis Khaan International Airport (airport code UBN) in Ulaanbaatar replaced the "old" airport (airport code ULN) in 2021. The airport is approximately 50 km (31 miles) south of the city, and airport shuttles, city buses, Ubers, and taxis are all available.

There are three banks with ATMs in the Chinggis Khaan airport. Airport banks have a reputation for not giving the best rates on currency exchanges, but I suppose convenience has its price. We did not use the airport banks since it was easy to find ATMs in the city.

LODGING

There were plenty of hotels and locations to be found on Airbnb in both Seoul and Ulaanbaatar, so finding a place to stay overnight was easy. Jon had been to Seoul a few times and liked the Hotel Hu Incheon Airport. It is a nice hotel that is reasonably priced and close enough to have a free airport shuttle.

For the first few days in Ulaanbaatar, we stayed in an apartment found through Olly and Goyo Travel. Our apartment was a few blocks from the downtown area near restaurants, markets, banks, and everything else we needed.

Outside Ulaanbaatar it is fairly easy to get a hotel even in a smaller town. Making a reservation in advance is not required. They may not be luxury accommodations, and some may not have hot water or indoor plumbing, but there will be a bed. It might not be a comfortable bed, but having an air mattress helps. The outhouse will be in the back.

In some of the more remote areas there may be Ger Camps, also called Tourist Camps. A ger is a round tent made with canvas over a wooden frame. They have been used by nomads for centuries. Some of these were better than the hotels. You can stay in a comfortable ger with a real bed and take a short walk to a washroom which might have hot water and showers. There is usually a main building housing a small restaurant with a limited menu. If you enjoy noodles and mutton (sheep) you may be in luck.

If all else failed, we also brought tents. My choice was a one-person backpacking tent, while Jon had a two-person "Big Agnes" tent, which, compared to mine, was spacious luxury.

COMMUNICATIONS

To state the obvious, if your phone doesn't operate in the places you intend to visit, then communications will be a problem. Mongolia does have internet availability in most places, and access to satellites is improving. The two largest phone companies in Mongolia are Mobicom and Unitel, which both provide 4G service. Many cell phone providers in the United States will offer travel plans for an additional fee. Check with your service provider for current plans.

Replacing the SIM (Subscriber Identity Module) card is another way to manage international phone calls. Every cellphone has a SIM card, which gives the phone its unique identity. There are thousands of phones out there exactly like yours, but only your SIM card is coded for your individual phone number. The SIM card is then linked to a phone service provider. Local SIM cards can be purchased in stores, airports, and online. SIM cards are standard size, so any card should fit any phone. SIM cards allow for voice calling, text and data usage up to the limits on the card purchased. They have nothing to do with the memory in the phone, such as photographs, contacts, or other stored data. Changing a SIM card will not delete anything from the phone. It simply gives the phone a new local phone number and cell carrier.

Newer phones may have an eSIM (embedded SIM) rather than a physical SIM card. An eSIM is a permanent part of the phone's software programming. There is no actual card to remove or replace. Theoretically, it should be easy to switch cell carriers in a foreign country by going into the phone's settings and reconfiguring the eSIM to a local carrier. This eliminates the need to buy a new SIM card. Some phones with eSIM technology may still have a tray for a physical SIM card. These are dual-SIM phones, which can accommodate two active SIMs. This allows for two phone numbers, each with a different carrier, on the same phone. My advice would be to visit a phone store before the trip for further details.

Wi-Fi hotspots are available but unpredictable. Most are hotels or "internet café" type businesses that offer either free or inexpensive Wi-Fi service. I have used WhatsApp and found it to be very reliable with Wi-Fi access. WhatsApp can also work without the internet by using the phone's cellular data. For my Verizon phone, I found cell service to be spotty at best. Wi-Fi access in Mongolia was surprisingly more available than I had originally thought, which was far better than just hoping there was a friendly cell tower nearby. Most of my communications home, whether it was voice or text, went through WhatsApp.

Signal is another great option for a free app that also uses end-to-end encryption for text, voice and even video calls. Having multiple options was comforting, although they both depend upon access to the internet.

Facebook messenger, text, and email are also good ways to send information that does not require an immediate response. Most communications we had with contacts in Mongolia before our trip were through email or FB messenger.

Satellite phones along with their monthly plans are great, but also very expensive. Even renting them runs into several hundred dollars. Luckily, Jon had a device that worked as a satellite phone. We thought this would be helpful if we had a need for emergency communications or GPS positioning. It worked well when we tested it before the trip. Unfortunately, it did not work at all in Mongolia. We believe it had trouble accessing the satellite.

POWER

Electricity in the United States is 110 volts. The electricity in Mongolia (and Europe) is 220 volts. These are not compatible with each other, so much so that the plugs for the wall sockets are different. 220-volt plugs have two round prongs, which are unlike the two flat prongs (and sometimes with one round ground) used for plugs in the United States.

My primary electrical need was to charge my cellphone. Most phone chargers are dual voltage, meaning they are compatible with either 110 or 220 voltages. The fine print on the charger will specify this. If the input states "100-240V~50-60Hz" then it can be used with either of the two voltages. The charger for my phone also states "Travel Adapter, Voltage Adapter" for further clarity. All that is needed is a travel adapter that has the European two round prong style that I can plug my charger into.

Do not expect to find many USB ports for phone charging. There might be some in the more upscale hotels in the big cities, but these are the exceptions.

VOLTAGE CONVERTER VS. TRAVEL ADAPTER

A voltage converter can plug into a 220V outlet and change the voltage to 110V. You can then plug 110V devices into the converter safely. A travel adapter only allows you to convert the plug configuration so that a different outlet design may be used. Travel adapters do not change the voltage. If the only need is to charge a cellphone, and it is dual voltage (as most are) then a travel adapter should suffice. A voltage converter would not be necessary. A voltage converter is only needed if the items to be used are single voltage 110V only, and not dual voltage.

SOLAR

Our trip would include very remote areas without a reliable electricity grid. Since the only electricity needed was to charge our phones, solar charging was a good option. Solar panels were secured to the packs on my bike's cargo rack. This generated electricity which was stored in batteries, called "bricks" or power banks. At night I could charge my phone by plugging it into the charged power bank. Since my phone was not just my means of communications home, but also my source for information, translation, weather, luggage location and various other things, I could not take a chance of my phone going down.

A word of caution – the Transportation Security Administration (TSA) has specific rules about what batteries can be brought on a commercial aircraft due to the risk of fire. Check with the TSA for the latest guidelines.

LANGUAGE

Mongolia uses the Cyrillic alphabet which has 35 characters and 13 vowels, which looks a bit like Klingon to me. It was introduced in 1946 during the days of Soviet Russian control, replacing the traditional vertical Mongolian script. Some letters are familiar, but others are just strange symbols that give no clue for pronunciation. I downloaded three key apps onto my phone: Google lens, Google translate, and Wola.io. With Google translate and Wola.io, I can type in English, and it can translate to Mongolian. Theoretically, if you have a Mongolian keyboard, it will translate Mongolian to English. I, however, did not have a Mongolian keyboard. This frustrated Mongolians trying to type answers to my questions. Google lens can take an image of Mongolian text and translate that into English. This came in handy for menus at restaurants.

In western Mongolia, there is a very strong Kazakh influence. Mongolia is completely surrounded by Russia to the north and China to the south. The western edge of Mongolia is separated from Kazakhstan by the 62-mile wide Russian-Chinese border. To me, both the Mongolian and Kazakh people and language appear very similar. However, both sides will let you know there are distinct differences. The Kazakh alphabet looks like Cyrillic but has 45 characters. It is unique enough that many Mongolians cannot speak or read Kazakh, and vice versa. Maybe it is like Spanish and Italian, kind of similar but distinctly different. By the end of the trip, I needed Google translate to understand Mongolian, Kazakh, Russian and Korean.

BIKES

Knowing that Mongolia has areas of unpaved roads and difficult terrain outside of Ulaanbaatar, we assumed mountain bikes would be the best choice. Buying bikes in Ulaanbaatar was less expensive and much easier than trying to ship our bikes over there.

Jon was in Seoul a few months before our trip and was able to visit Ulaanbaatar. He found the Alton Bike Shop and bought two mountain bikes, along with a few modifications such as more padded seats, hybrid tires, and spare tubes. We also wanted both bikes outfitted with rear pannier bags, water bottles and odometers. I bought pannier bags ahead of time and used them as carry-on bags for the flight. I also bought a solar powered odometer small enough to stuff in a bag so I could bring it home with me.

Olly at Goyo Travel allowed us to store our bikes at their business until we arrived. They do mountain biking expeditions and have a large storage room full of bikes and outdoor gear. It was yet another act of kindness Olly extended to us.

WEATHER

Mongolia is known for its brutal weather. Ulaanbaatar has the infamous distinction as the world's coldest capital city. Winter temperatures can drop as low as -25°C to -40°C (-13°F to -40°F) and can be even colder in the high elevations of the Altai Mountains, where we plan to end our trip by early October. Weather preparation was vitally important!

Weather information was easily found on internet searches, and we also downloaded weather apps onto our phones. Although this was great for general information, there were many times when the local weather we experienced was different from what the weather app reported. We expected to begin our trip with daily high temperatures around 50-60°F, with lows in the mid 30's, according to the "average" September weather along our route. Average rainfall in September is around 23 mm (less than one inch) for the month. The mostly westerly winds can gust from 8-11 mph, which means there is potential for headwinds most of the way. We also expected the weather to become significantly colder as we moved further west into the Altai Mountain range.

Being a Florida guy for over 30 years, I was concerned about sleeping outside in a tent during freezing weather. February in Tennessee brought some cold nights, so I set up my tent on the back deck and camped out. I quickly found out that a sleeping bag rated for 20-degrees is not as warm as one might think. I bought a fleece liner online which added just enough warmth. After a few more cold nights on the back deck to tweak my gear, I discovered my sleeping bag with a fleece liner, along with a sleeping pad, thermal underwear, pants, one shirt, one fleece sweatshirt, two pairs of wool hiking socks and a wool cap could keep me mostly comfortable on a 23°F night.

Weather issues have become an increasing concern for Mongolia, especially over the past few years. A weather phenomenon known as a "Dzud" produces hot dry summers followed by brutally cold winters with increased snowfall. The dry summer conditions reduce the amount of grass for grazing. Livestock will eat whatever grass is available, further depleting the supply. When the harsh winter weather arrives, primarily out of Siberia, the minimal remaining grass is buried under ice and snow. Without access to adequate grazing, millions of livestock succumb to both freezing and starvation. This is devastating in a country where one third of the population makes a living by herding or agriculture. Climate change, once again, seems to be the cause.

FOOD

Ulaanbaatar was quite urban and had everything we needed, such as supermarkets and restaurants. Outside of the city, we needed to be more self-reliant. A key piece of information would be the availability of markets. Since I could not find good information about this, I turned to a group on Facebook: *Traveling to Beautiful Mongolia & The Mongol World.* My wife found this group, and it turned out to be a wealth of information provided by locals and those who had traveled to Mongolia. They reassured us that yes, there are markets along the way, averaging about every 30-40 km. It was unclear just what kind of markets there were, but we expected to buy enough food to get us by.

The typical Mongolian breakfast consists of fried dough or biscuits with yak butter and tea. Fruits and vegetables are not common. The climate is very dry and brutally cold over the winter. Crops are difficult to tend with a nomadic lifestyle and a growing season of maybe three months at the most. Agriculture in some areas has begun to improve recently with the building of greenhouses. This can extend the growing season by an additional month or two.

Meats are common in the Mongolian diet, sourced mostly from the "five snouts" consisting of cow/yak, sheep (mutton), goat, camel, and horse. The main meal is served in the evening, commonly meat served with noodles or rice, along with milk tea.

The Mongolian diet is not known for being a healthy one. The meat-heavy diet along with a lack of vegetables has been associated with a high incidence of chronic disease. Mongolia has some of the highest mortality rates in the world due to cardiovascular disease, obesity, type 2 diabetes, anemia, and vitamin D deficiency.

WATER

Essential for life, water is an extremely important consideration. I have heard of the rule of 3's – you can live 3 minutes without air, 3 days without water and 3 weeks without food. My guess was that Mongolia had plenty of air, and we should encounter enough markets along the way to resupply our food. Water sources may be unpredictable, so we plan to carry a good supply with us. Bottled water is a good choice. I also have a backpack with a pouch for a 3-liter water bladder, along with two 2.5-liter CamelBaks and two aluminum water bottles.

I would never trust the water purity of streams or ponds without sanitizing it first. I must assume that there are harmful microorganisms like bacteria (responsible for 80-90% of traveler's diarrhea), viruses (norovirus, rotavirus), protozoa (giardia, cryptosporidium) or other waterborne pathogens. At the very least this could cause vomiting and diarrhea, with the potential for much worse. Standard advice of "boil it, cook it, peel it or forget it" is still helpful. Traveler's diarrhea is most commonly caused by poor hygiene practices, not only by the individual, but also by those preparing the food. Restaurant food is not always guaranteed to be safe, and food from street vendors is even less so. Even local tap water can potentially contain harmful microorganisms. Just because it is water from a hotel does not mean it is guaranteed safe. Common things like ice in a drink, wetting a toothbrush, or getting shower water in the mouth can be enough to cause illness.

Fortunately, water purification is easy. I used the Sawyer Squeeze filtration system, which consists of a 32oz water collection bag with tubing to run through a filter. This removes over 99% of all bacteria and protozoa, along with microplastics. That alone should be adequate, but I also have Aquatabs purification tablets. These also cover essentially all bacteria and protozoa, and in addition protect against viruses. One 49mg tablet is enough for up to 3 liters, which is exactly the size of my water containers. Boiling is another good option. A rolling boil for one minute is usually enough to sterilize water. If above 2,000m (6,500 feet) elevation, then a three-minute boil is recommended.

HEALTH

Before going on any trips out of the country, I always check the Center for Disease Control website (cdc.gov/travel) for travel advisories and health precautions. By entering your destination country in the search bar (Mongolia, for example) you can see what preparations are needed. I was pleased to see that there were no travel advisories for Mongolia, and just routine vaccines, including Hepatitis A, were recommended. I suggest checking this early on since the Hepatitis A vaccine is a series of two shots spaced 6 months apart. One is not fully protected until a few weeks after the second vaccine is given. This should be completed before the travel date.

The CDC website also has suggestions for a "Healthy Travel Packing List" specific for different countries including items like water purification methods, antidiarrheal medications, insect repellant, sunscreen, hand sanitizer, and many things one might not think about until you realize you don't have it. Specific medical needs like spare eyeglasses, prescription medications, medical devices, and documents are also important.

I also thought it was a good idea to bring some antibiotics in case one of us developed severe traveler's diarrhea not improved by Pepto-Bismol. Bacteria (salmonella, shigella, campylobacter, and some strains of E. coli) are the most common causes, so I had both Zithromax (azithromycin) and Septra (sulfamethoxazole/trimethoprim) as suggested by the CDC website. My local primary care provider was kind enough to prescribe them when I told him about my trip and asked for them. I told him I would only use them if indicated by CDC guidelines. Fortunately, most episodes of traveler's diarrhea are self-limited and do not require treatment with antibiotics.

PHYSICAL PREPARATION

I think the best preparation is a healthy lifestyle. In my time as a pediatrician, I was always chanting the mantra about the benefits of exercise and a healthy diet. In our family, it was just normal to live that way. I have always believed in the benefits of aerobic conditioning. Strength training with weights certainly has its place, but the cardiovascular fitness gained from aerobic conditioning is crucial to good health. Walking, running, biking, and swimming are great examples. If you have access to exercise equipment or a gym, ellipticals, treadmills, and stationary bikes are great. Breaking a sweat in air-conditioned comfort just seems a lot easier. But, since this adventure is a bike trip, riding a bike seemed like a logical thing to do. One of the first things I did after moving to Tennessee was to buy a mountain bike. There is just something natural about being out in the woods, and seeing an occasional deer is like bonus points!

Another benefit of healthy cardiovascular fitness is improved endurance. We planned to ride bikes an average of thirty miles daily for six weeks. I did not want to be forced to quit early because I was not physically prepared. The goal was to work my thighs for strength and do cardio for endurance. The training I did was not just for the trip, but also because I just enjoy working out. I do it primarily for the long-term health benefits, along with simply having fun.

MENTAL PREPARATION

"90% of baseball is half mental"
—Yogi Berra

I quickly concluded that most of what concerned me about this trip was the large degree of things I did not know. After agreeing to go with Jon, with the great adventure component that I could not pass up, I felt a degree of anxiety developing. I will be leaving my safe and secure world and going on a risky venture that is potentially dangerous. I have a wife and two kids that I love very much and would like to see again. There was no one I could find who had done a trip like this before, so no trailblazer to follow. This is completely on us, mistakes and all. What am I getting myself into?

I have the amazing good fortune of being married to a mental health professional. As a licensed clinical social worker (LCSW) Val has vast experience in cognitive behavioral therapy. Over the years, I have heard her advise that "What you think determines how you feel." I took this to heart. The excitement about the adventure and beauty Jon and I were going to encounter far outweighed any hesitation I might have. I found myself thinking about the trip daily, both the fun things and the more arduous. My imagination put me in Mongolia. I sought out potential problems, then tried to create solutions. I tried to think of every disaster that we might encounter. Some things, like stocking up on food, water, proper clothing, etc. were things I could anticipate and plan for accordingly. Other things, like weather, medical issues, mechanical problems, insects, unfriendly wildlife, etc., might be out of my control. It was impossible to anticipate everything, but I wanted to be prepared for any realistic problems that we might encounter.

Situational anxiety of the unknown can be helped by reducing the unknowns. This involves researching questions as they come up and finding solutions. I spent a great deal of time on the internet seeking answers to my questions. I began with the basics – food, shelter, and clothing. I found that even though Mongolia has vast areas that are sparsely populated, the best chance of finding people, and not getting lost, was to stay on the roads. Roads connect villages, and villages have people who need basic necessities. I learned there are occasional hotels and more markets than I thought. Slowly but surely, I could feel bursts of empowerment by overcoming obstacles.

PART TWO

The Journey

> *"A journey of a thousand miles begins with the first pedal"*
> *—Lao Tzu (sort of)*

AUGUST 21, 2023: GOING TO SAN FRANCISCO

My phone went off at 1:39 a.m. A text message from the airline said there was a delay in my 7:00 a.m. flight to San Francisco, and to contact the airline. I called the airline, and the friendly customer service representative provided me with a new arrival time in San Francisco. My quick sleepy math calculated a 16-minute transfer to catch the connecting flight to Seoul. There was a minimal chance I could make that, and zero chance my bag would. The customer service agent gave me a few options, each one worse than the one before. I might still get to Seoul on the afternoon of August 22, but that means taking a flight connecting through Osaka, Japan to a different airline. The thought of going through baggage claims, customs, and then immediately going into the security screening line again did not sound like a viable option. More complications create more chances for problems.

After a two-hour phone call with airline customer service, the best (or least bad) idea was to take the later flight which arrived in San Francisco at 9:24 p.m. This provided plenty of time to make the last flight out of San Francisco just before midnight (August 21) arriving in Seoul at 4:20 a.m. (August 23) after crossing nine time zones and the International Date Line somewhere out in the Pacific Ocean. That provided me 10 hours to make the next flight to Ulaanbaatar. The downside was trying to get some sleep. The original plan was for Jon and me to arrive early enough to get a hotel room near the airport so we could get some rest before the flight to Ulaanbaatar and, perhaps more importantly, adjust to the time difference. A nice overnight hotel stay in Seoul was no longer a possibility. The Seoul Incheon International Airport has a spa on the lowest floor with sleep areas, showers, and a sauna. I guess things could have been worse. The first rule of travel: expect the unexpected and be flexible about it.

My new flight to San Francisco left in the evening which gave me another 12 hours at home before going to the airport. I thought that it was a nice gift to have some extra time with Val and our dog Ziggy. Although I was happy to have more time, the day had a bit of a weird ominous feeling. I think we both were emotionally prepared to say goodbye earlier, then had to spend the whole day thinking about it. I was leaving for two months without being fully able to know what possible hazards, if any, that Jon and I might face. I loved my life at home with Val, as we had both shed responsibilities and enjoyed our new retired life. There was a nagging worry this trip would somehow ruin it all if something bad happened. This would either be a grand adventure or a potential disaster.

The time eventually came to make the trip to the airport. It was a 45-minute drive for Val and me, along with Ziggy and a large "white elephant" kind of weird feeling that I could be heading into any number of dangerous situations in extremely remote areas halfway around the world. We arrived at the airport and headed to the departure lane. I had a large backpack, a small backpack, and a bag for camping gear that I took out of the car and placed by the curb. I was wondering if going on this trip was the right decision, but it was a little late to back out now. We had a long embrace, and I think we both had a tear in our eyes. It was about then that the parking security guy came over to yell at us for taking too much time. Those guys can be so annoying... Val and I had one last kiss, and I had to let her go. I stepped on the curb as she got back into the car and drove away. I had an empty feeling as I watched her disappear. After the car vanished, I stared at the spot where I last saw her. With an intense feeling of loneliness, I picked up the packs and went inside to find the security screening area and my departure gate for San Francisco.

It was a relatively short wait until the boarding process began. We took off on time and the person sitting next to me immediately put their earbuds in and fell asleep. That was fine with me as I was not really in a talking mood. The window seat gave me a terrific view of a beautiful sunset. A glowing band of bright yellow-orange was sandwiched between the dark ground and purple-blue clouds. After the sunlight faded, it was difficult to make out any features on the ground. We would be crossing the Rocky Mountains, and I wondered how they would compare to the Mongolian mountains. Although it had only been a couple of hours, I already missed Val and Ziggy. Two months was a long time to be away. The reality of what I was doing began to set in.

Last glimmer of sun on the way to San Francisco

We arrived in San Francisco right on time. Going through the airport was easy and I quickly found my departure gate for the flight to Seoul. It was great moving around with only the small backpack. The large backpack and camping gear bag were in checked baggage, and the luggage tracker confirmed that the backpack arrived with me. Looking around the departure gate waiting area, there was an interesting variety of people. I tried to guess where people were from, although I had no way to know for sure. We were going to Seoul, so I assumed there were many Koreans on the flight.

AUGUST 22-23: SEOUL

Just before midnight we began the 13-hour flight to Seoul. I enjoyed the dinner served and found a dumb movie to watch on the small seatback screen. I was lucky to have a three-seat row to myself and made a mini bed out of it. It was lumpy, and I couldn't stretch out, but it was better than sitting upright in a cramped seat. Flying over the Pacific Ocean at night helped as there was only blackness outside the window. The long flight threw my sleep cycle completely off, but I was not as tired as I thought I would be. The first land mass we crossed was Japan. In the darkness, around 3-something in the morning, I saw clusters of lights indicating a large city. Judging by the flight map on the seatback screen, I determined that it had to be Tokyo. A short time later the plane landed in Seoul. It was early in the morning of August 23 and still dark outside.

The Seoul Incheon International Airport was large and modern, with shining white tile floors that were spotless. The departures floor had 16 rows of counters shared by different airlines simply by changing the logos on the electronic signs behind them. Many were Asian airlines that I had not heard of before. On the fourth floor there were plenty of restaurants, which was a good thing since I had loads of time and liked to eat. With my bags on a luggage cart, I was free to explore. It was an extremely busy place with people going everywhere even in the very early morning hours. I found some quiet sitting areas that I thought might be good for a nap and tried to make up for the lack of sleep on the plane. Considering it was midafternoon at home, I was not as tired as I thought. Real sleep would not come until after I made it to Ulaanbaatar.

Jon arrived in Seoul the previous day, the day I was originally supposed to arrive before my flight delays. He stayed at the Hotel Hu, a short Uber ride away from the airport. Jon texted me mid-morning saying he was coming to the airport to meet up. I had this strange thought, "Gee, I hope I can recognize him!" I had only met him once, just briefly. Over the last few months, we had some video calls planning for the trip, which helped. I thought I could narrow it down as there were not many American looking travelers in the airport. Then I spotted a guy wearing a Green Bay Packers hat with two large duffel bags, looking like someone ready for a long expedition. That had to be Jon. I found out later that he did not recognize me at first. But, I was happy to see him and glad he arrived on time. The big smile on his face was reassuring. I thought it odd that this long and potentially dangerous trip, which would require a great deal of teamwork, was undertaken by two guys who barely knew each other. It was a huge leap of faith, but I trusted him and was pleased I was not in this situation alone. I had thought about what I would do if for some reason he never arrived. That would have been a problem...

We checked in together for our Miat-Mongolian Airlines flight to Ulaanbaatar. There are large signs at the front of the airport lobby showing all flights and the row where their ticket agents could be found. Once the correct row is found, the airline name is posted at their counter. We knew what their logo looked like but having the signage in both Mongolian and English also helped. The woman at the Miat-Mongolian Airlines counter checked in Jon's two bags first, tagging one in Jon's name and one in mine. We realized the error but did not think it was anything to worry about.

We then went through the passport security screening process. The very long lines made for an incredibly slow journey, eventually coming to the small podium where the passport officer stood. Jon went first and breezed right through. My passport was scanned next, and a red light lit up. I immediately thought "This can't be good!" I was told to get out of line and go to the Security Office. There was no explanation of what the problem was, or where the Security Office was, since all the signs were in Korean. After checking around, I was directed to a non-descript door whose only sign said, "In Progress." After staring at the door not knowing what to do, it opened, and I was escorted inside by two uniformed security officers to a small room with several pieces of luggage. In broken English, the security officer asked me if this was my bag. Recognizing Jon's bag, I thought the easy answer was "yes." I was asked if I had "anything illegal" inside, and I said I didn't think so. I immediately thought Jon better not be trying to smuggle in some weed, or something worse! I really did not think he would, but they pulled me out of the line for some reason. The two officers gently unpacked the bag, examining everything closely. He then asked if I had any lighters. Since this was the bag with all of Jon's camping gear, it was likely there were lighters inside, but I did not know for sure. After several long minutes, there emerged not one, but two small lighters that the officers proudly displayed. Apparently one lighter is OK but not two. I apologized for not knowing the rules and they let me go, without the lighters. I was quite happy that Jon had nothing else illegal in his bag.

Grateful to be free and clear, I now returned to the long, slow passport security screening lines again. I was glad we had started this process hours before our scheduled departure time. The plane was not going to wait for me because I was detained by security. Fortunately, I had better luck this time when I reached the security officer. The officer scanned my passport and, without any red lights, allowed me to go through. Jon was waiting for me on the other side of the security area with a concerned look. I told him I had some good news and some bad news... The good news was that it was his bag. The bad news was that he is out two lighters. We both laughed a nervous laugh. Overall, it was a minor problem. I do have to give credit to the airport security personnel. They were polite, careful, and considerate of Jon's things as they unpacked and neatly repacked his bag. Their job is to keep us all safe, and I applaud them for their efforts. Not getting arrested was a bonus!

The extra time it took to get through security did not matter as the flight to Ulaanbaatar was also significantly delayed. With loads of time to sit, Jon gave me a book to read about Mongolia. I started with Chapter 4 – "Making Friends." I had just begun the second page when a voice asked me where I was going. 11-year-old Bayanmunkh was sitting next to me, speaking in clear English. On first impression, I immediately liked my young Mongolian friend. His face was kind with a warm smile. He was neatly dressed just like any 11-year-old in the US. I could tell he really enjoyed speaking English. I told him I was going to Ulaanbaatar, and he said he lived there with his parents and older sister. We had a wonderful conversation about Mongolia, family, school, and life, with Bayanmunkh smiling the entire time. His sister taught him how to speak English and did a terrific job. He said the best thing about school was his friends, and the worst was homework. I guess some things are universal. He offered to give me his phone number in case I needed him to translate something for me. I politely declined but thanked him for his kind offer. I was so happy that the first friend I met on this trip was Bayanmunkh. What a great kid!

The almost four-hour flight to Ulaanbaatar was uneventful. The Seoul Incheon Airport is on the western coast of Korea. Immediately after takeoff we were over the Yellow Sea. Our flight path then took us over China. The grassy mountainous terrain was devoid of trees and showed no signs of civilization. We flew near Beijing, but it was on the opposite side of the plane and out of view. There was nothing I could see to make me think we are over either China or Mongolia. It all looked the same from the air.

Flying over rural China

Sometime later the flight crew announced, in both Mongolian and English, that we were preparing to land. I caught a glimpse of Ulaanbaatar as we made our landing approach. It was now late in the evening with the sun low in the sky. That same sun would soon be coming up at home. There were several windmills just outside the city. I thought this was a great place for windmills, on top of the mountains surrounding the largest city in Mongolia. From the air, I saw well defined city limits. Within the city there are densely packed areas of housing with many buildings, some quite tall. Outside the city there were large tracts of empty land. It seemed ironic that Mongolians, known for living as independent nomads, would be so condensed into one huge urban city. With a population of over 1.3 million people in Ulaanbaatar, about half of the entire country lives in this one city.

We had a smooth landing, deplaned, and headed for Customs. The officer in the booth spoke English well, making the screening much easier. Chinggis Khaan International Airport, which is the only international airport in Mongolia, is clean and modern, although much smaller than the airport in Seoul. Signage in both Mongolian and English helped us find our way.

Olly from Goyo Travel was very helpful in arranging a place to stay. We met Olly's driver at the baggage terminal, right on schedule, and were happy he spoke some English. The only issue was finding the apartment. Ulaanbaatar is like most other large cities, with traffic congestion and occasional graffiti spray-painted on buildings. But it also has art, music, and sports arenas. There were a few signs in English, but most by far were in Mongolian. I enjoyed seeing the city as we drove, but I also had been awake for too many hours and wanted to get some sleep. The driver rode around, made some phone calls, and rode around some more. I knew the driver was a local, and he knew the territory, but all the buildings looked the same to me, each one just as drab and nondescript as the other. Finally, he found the correct building, but he did not know which apartment was ours. He then tried several doors until he found one that fit the key. We were happy when we finally entered the two-bedroom apartment. It was convenient for everything we wanted in the city. Now it was time to unpack a little, find some food, and get some sleep. Flight delays, customs lines, and getting lost made for a very long day as we arrived hours later than expected.

There was a small restaurant near the apartment with good food and Wi-Fi. I finally had a chance to call home! I knew with my delayed arrival time that Val would probably be awake. When she answered the phone, she was not the usual cheerful person I expected. She sounded scared and upset. It seemed that my phone call, six hours later than expected, was the end of a nightmare. Flight tracking apps have their pros and cons. Val had awakened early and checked her FlightAware app to verify my plane's flight path. She saw the little plane's route leave the Seoul Airport and track over the Yellow Sea, but then it disappeared into darkness. China was blacked out with no cities or landmarks labeled. It was one empty mass where the flight line stopped, well short of Ulaanbaatar. At first, she thought "Oh, it's just a glitch" but when minutes turned into hours she began to think "What if he was forced down or crashed in China?" With no helpful information online, she watched the news terrified of what she might see.

I immediately remembered our conversations during the planning for this trip. We discussed risks and the possibility of real danger, even life-threatening danger. We both had considered the possibility I might not come home. As the phone call progressed, I finally heard Val's voice relax, knowing that Jon and I were safe. I knew my adventure trek wouldn't be easy for her. I thought about how I would feel if our roles were reversed. I could only imagine how stressful those hours were. It must have been a horrible, scary feeling for her, with the lack of information only making things worse. Being so far away, all she could do was worry. Even though everything turned out well, I was left shaken by the thought of "What if it hadn't turned out well?" I told myself not to forget that feeling, and how vital communication would be as the trip progressed.

AUGUST 24: ULAANBAATAR

We stayed in Ulaanbaatar for a couple of days so that we could get over the jetlag, stock up on supplies, and obtain cash at the ATMs. It was good to sleep late and try to adjust to the local time. Olly had a few basic breakfast items ready for us. The apartment had a kitchen, and the refrigerator had eggs, juice, bread, butter, and a few other essentials. This was helpful since we had not yet ventured out to find where all the restaurants were.

After a quick breakfast, the first thing we did was to get some cash at the ATM. It felt like it was a big deal getting 500,000 Tugriks but I came back to reality knowing that it was only $145 USD. We then walked several blocks to Goyo Travel to pick up the bikes that they had been storing for us.

I can't say enough good things about Olly and Goyo. They helped us out numerous times by arranging airfare, finding lodging, and answering seemingly countless email questions. I was very happy to finally meet them both. Olly is English and his wife Goyo is Mongolian. We spent more time talking with Olly as English is his primary language. I enjoyed hearing his British accent. Olly looked to be in his 40's with a thin build and small moustache. He appeared to be in good shape, probably from going on all those mountain bike tours. Goyo spoke limited English and seemed to be the businessperson of the relationship, being very pleasant but more serious than Olly. I guessed that was why the business was named after her. Along with picking up our bikes, Goyo gave me a quick tutorial on SIM cards and how to use it in my phone. She loaned me a local SIM card and loaded it with data, giving me several options for phone and internet service which should work anywhere in Mongolia (hopefully...)

Goyo was also able to register us with Mongolian Immigration. All visitors staying longer than 30 days must register with the local immigration office. The process was easy, just filling out a form with our passport numbers. This saved us from a trip to the immigration office and prevented problems upon leaving the country.

The next place we went was the Alton Bike Shop. Alton is a Korean brand I was unfamiliar with but seemed to be popular there. To me, our bikes were something of a hybrid between a durable mountain bike and a nicer riding gravel bike. Given the long hours of riding, I was happy we opted for the upgraded "saddle" or bike seat. In hindsight, I think the better seat along with padded bike shorts saved my butt! I liked the bike and wanted to add a heavy-duty cargo rack and get a few more spare tire tubes. At the bike shop we met Bimba, who said her cousin owned the store. She was in charge while her cousin was out for the day. Bimba was probably in her mid-30's, a little heavy-set, with classic Mongolian facial features (rounded face, prominent cheekbones) along with a beautiful smile. We explained our plan to bike from Ulaanbaatar to Ulgii. She was quite interested in our trip since she had family in Ulgii. Bimba was very generous, giving us things from her cousin's shop like free tire tubes, water bottles, neck gaiters, an air pump, and a few other goodies. She also gave us a quick lesson about important Mongolian skills, like how to approach a ger without being attacked by the dog. The key is loudly yelling "hold the dog!" before you get too close. Unfortunately, I could not remember how to say it in Mongolian. This amazing woman spoke Mongolian, Russian, German, and English. As we left, she made sure we had contact information for the store in case we needed any help during our trip.

Having bikes improved our ability to get around, but city traffic was always an issue. The streets were busy, and at times I felt like I was biking in downtown Manhattan. A wide median in a main boulevard had prominent statues of a Mongol rider on horseback leading camels laden with cargo. We rode to Sukhbaatar Square, a large public area with a huge statue of Chinggis Khaan seated while looking over his vast domain. Monuments, streets, and gardens are named after their still revered national hero. A few very old-looking Asian style buildings seemed swallowed by the larger, more modern buildings surrounding them.

Sukhbaatar Square, Ulaanbaatar

Streets of Ulaanbaatar

Several blocks away was a statue of the four Beatles against a brick red apple background. There they were, John, Paul, George, and Ringo! As a Beatles fan it caught my attention. Although Western culture was banned under the Soviet control of Mongolia, young people often gathered in secret to share music and other symbols of freedom and democracy. After Mongolia became independent, statues of Lenin were destroyed. The Beatles statue represented all the art, music, and culture that served to inspire the independence movement.

The rest of the afternoon consisted of biking around the city, doing a little sightseeing, and looking for markets, restaurants, and ATMs. It was much easier getting around with the bikes as long as we were careful with the crazy city traffic. The streets were crowded with cars, trucks, and buses. Dust and diesel fumes were a bit much at times, but the larger concern was to avoid getting hit by a careless driver. They had standard traffic lights and stop signs, and most (but not all) drivers followed the rules of the road.

We enjoyed meeting locals who would say "hello" in English knowing that we were Western tourists. For some, that was the extent of their English vocabulary. Others were fluent and helped with answers to our questions. Restaurants were plentiful, and the food was tasty and inexpensive. Lunch for two, including two beers, was $13 USD.

We arrived back at the apartment early enough to work on our bikes. Jon brought a small trailer with him which attached to his bike's rear axle. This made the daily chore of packing up both quick and easy. Jon stuffed his gear in a duffel bag and put it in the trailer. I, on the other hand, strapped my backpack and gear bag to the rear cargo rack on my bike. I had spent considerable time before the trip experimenting on how to strap a large backpack securely to a relatively small cargo rack. I made a cargo rack extension out of scrap wood I had at home, drilling holes so that I was sure I could fit it to any rack using cable ties. I had to put a hinge on it so that it would fit in the backpack for travel. Ratcheting tie down straps completed the process. It was lightweight, secure, and worked well overall. The downside was that getting the straps just right each day became time-consuming. I am sure the time I wasted every morning fooling around with this eventually became annoying to Jon but, to his credit, he never said a word about it.

That evening we treated Goyo and Olly to dinner to thank them for their help. Our conversations up to that point had been brief, addressing specific questions. It was nice to have a chat with friends over wine and dinner. Olly could speak Mongolian but even after living there for several years, he still struggled at times with the language. That was certainly understandable considering how completely different the English and

Mongolian languages were. Besides being language tutors for each other, Olly and Goyo were well matched. They both seemed to enjoy each other, along with the daily adventures they had with tourists. They live in Mongolia during the busy tourist season then go back to England in the winter. Their three young children were still in school, unsure if they would eventually be a part of their parents' business. Living in both England and Mongolia, their children must have an interesting life, in two very diverse worlds. I imagined a world of opportunity for their futures.

AUGUST 25: THE BLACK MARKET

This was our last chance to make final preparations before we began our bike trip the following morning. We went to several ATMs but all of them declined our cards. The cards had worked previously, and I had given my bank at home a travel notice, so I did not understand why the cards were declined. This could be a major problem if we were unable to access any cash. We went back to the same ATM we had used the day before and luckily everything worked fine. Maybe certain banks or ATMs were just unable to take my card. I was relieved and happy to get some cash. I knew I would need it.

There was a large store on a busy street corner with the sign "Hypermart" over the door. I assumed that was a different translation for "supermarket." This looked like an opportunity to purchase our last-minute food items. The Hypermart was as clean and well-stocked as any supermarket I had seen back home. It took some effort to locate items since the signs were in Mongolian and many of the products had Russian or Korean packaging. I managed to find food that would keep well for several days and was easy to prepare. I bought oatmeal, raisins, tea, honey, fruit, pasta, tomato sauce (that seemed more like spicy ketchup than tomato sauce,) canned tuna, and several other items that I carried in the pannier bags.

A large "Black Market" was also nearby with lots of bargains on loads of items for sale. Black markets originally had the reputation of dealing in secret sales of illegal goods. Bargains could be had with no questions asked. Although they are still called "black markets" they are no longer secret or illegal. Around the outside of the market area were shipping containers lined up side by side. Some were open and stuffed full of clothes, shoes, or whatever else that particular vendor sold. There was a central area of booths, mostly covered by canvas tarps or corrugated metal. I assumed there was a logical plan to it all, but it looked like a maze of random goods. There were mostly household items along with food, clothes, shoes, slippers, jackets, leather goods, horse saddles, musical instruments, knives, and countless other items. The small alleys between the booths were full of people. It gave me that "salmon swimming upstream" kind of feeling. Several locals greeted the Western looking tourists by giving us a smile and a nod. I bought a few Christmas gifts for Val and the kids.

While walking down a crowded area, a man walked in front of me and tried to grab the reading glasses out of my shirt pocket. His hand was pulling out the glasses when I grabbed his wrist. I had a moment of "what do I do now?" when I saw the surprised look on his face. I guess I was faster than he thought. He pulled away, and I let him go. I didn't know what his life was like, but I hoped that was not how he made a living. He wasn't a very good pickpocket. I remembered to put my wallet in the front pocket and also carry the backpack in front. It's more difficult to steal things that way.

Tomorrow the bike trek would begin, assuming that we safely made it out of the city traffic. Tonight might be our last hot shower, restaurant food, and comfortable bed for a while. I was looking forward to starting our biking while at the same time having a bit of trepidation about venturing into the unknown. The physical challenge of biking 30 miles a day did not bother me. I thought that would be the easy part, except for the mountains of course! It was the unknown things we might encounter that could be a problem. Adventure was calling, and I just hoped I was up to the challenge.

The Black Market in Ulaanbaatar

Jon (blue shirt on right) looking for Black Market deals

AUGUST 26: BIKING DAY 1 – ULAANBAATAR TO NALGAR GER CAMP – 29.8 MILES

We had a late start getting out of Ulaanbaatar. First came breakfast at a restaurant not far from our apartment. I had the "All American" consisting of scrambled eggs, toast, broccoli, carrots, and a hot dog. I am guessing it was the hot dog that made it "All American." They offered "seabuckthorn" juice, which was new to me. It looked a bit like orange juice but not as sweet. I enjoyed it, and it was something I looked forward to trying again.

Next was packing the gear, which always seemed to take longer than expected. My method was to strap my packs down on the bike's rear cargo rack, making sure they were balanced properly and secured enough not to spill out all over the road. Getting the tie-down straps just right took the most time. The kickstand was a big help to steady the bike while I loaded the packs and strapped them down. It was something I had not thought of for a mountain bike, but glad to have it. Jon had an easier time getting ready for the day. He loaded his gear into two duffel bags and put them in the bike trailer. Done. Very simple, and very fast.

Jon's trailer had one very cool feature. He had a tall, flexible pole at the back with colored flags on it. These were Tibetan prayer flags he obtained on his last trip to Nepal. Each color had a significant meaning, which represents the five basic "elements" – Blue symbolizes the sky and space, White symbolizes air, wind, clouds, and (according to some people we spoke to) mother's milk, Red symbolizes fire, Green symbolizes water, and Yellow symbolizes earth. The flags are considered sacred, and Buddhists believe as the prayer flags blow and fray in the wind, peace, wisdom, and compassion are spread to all beings.

While I was packing, and Jon was waiting, a local Mongolian man who spoke some English began a conversation with Jon. He seemed like a nice person, curious about the two tourists so far from home. Shortly after, a second man staggered up who appeared to be drunk. I could not understand what he was saying, but it sounded like he was slurring his words. The local man tried to keep him away from us. I thought he was either trying to protect us from erratic behavior or did not want us to get any negative impressions of the Mongolian people. The drunk man, however, seemed insistent on talking to us. A third man observing the situation joined in to help. They were both able to redirect the impaired man just long enough for us to get on the bikes and pedal away.

Day one of a long journey

The paved main road heading west out of Ulaanbaatar was busy, with three lanes of traffic in each direction. It is named Peace Avenue, which was anything but peaceful. Trucks would pass by close enough that I could reach out and touch them. The traffic, dust, and diesel fumes were reminders that city life and country life were different worlds. It took several miles, but eventually the traffic thinned as we put distance between us and the city. I was happy to finally make it out of the awful city traffic, where the rules of the road are at times just mere suggestions. The occasional running of red lights and ignoring pedestrians in crosswalks kept us bikers on our toes. Now we began to see rolling hills that stretched out forever. We were finally able to relax a little and enjoy the sunny 70-degree day.

Jon knew of a Buddhist monastery on the edge of town that he wanted to visit. We were told most of the monasteries, many being centuries old, were destroyed during the days of communism and Soviet control over Mongolia in the late 1930s to 1950s. Joseph Stalin ordered a purge where up to 90% of Buddhist monasteries in Mongolia were destroyed. Tragically, many sites were bombed, and untold numbers of monks were killed. Ironically, it was Stalin who eventually stopped the destruction as a gesture to show the West that the Soviets tolerated religious freedoms. This is just one of many reasons why Stalin has a legacy of being an evil monster.

We came upon the monastery and saw two buildings, a small older one beside a beautiful larger building that looked relatively new. Both buildings were made of brick with yellow and red trim. The entry door had very ornate, intricate designs in several colors. We cautiously approached the new building and saw there was one monk inside who nodded approval for us to enter. He then began prayer chants seated at a red bench while we quietly walked around. There were hundreds of Buddha statues, some being quite large, in cases along the walls. Jon had been to Tibet and explained some of the Buddhist relics we saw. Very ornate images were painted on the walls and ceiling, suggesting deep meaning and symbolism unknown to me. I was impressed by the colors - brightly painted orange, blue, white, green, and red throughout. The floor was shining with white marble tiles. Walking around, there was a powerful aura of respect for this holy place. I had never been to a Buddhist monastery before, and it gave me a sense of awe and admiration. I did not know if taking pictures was appropriate, but I also could not resist. I thought if my phone was on silent mode, avoiding the camera click sound, that it would not disturb the tranquility we were experiencing. I snuck in a few discreet shots and left a few tugriks in the collection basket. As we left, the monk continued his chants with no notice of our leaving.

Jon (on left) inside the Buddhist monastery

Beautifully ornate and spotlessly clean with vibrant colors

We continued with our trip out of the city, pleased that the traffic had decreased but not so happy biking up hills loaded with 75lbs of gear and supplies. Jon seemed to do well with his small trailer, but the two packs on the rear cargo rack caused my bike to be top-heavy, which made quick turns difficult. The flat stretches of paved road were wonderful, but the hills were a challenge. We climbed about 1,000 feet in elevation and, yes, we did walk the bikes up some of the steeper grades. At the top of a long grade there was a tall vertical pole extending from a round pile of rocks. The pole was covered in what looked like scraps of cloth, mostly blue. It looked significant, but I did not know the meaning behind it (yet...)

Many cars passing us waved or gave us the 'thumbs up' sign, smiling approval. I didn't think they saw many bikers that far out from the city. Toyota was a popular car brand, making up the majority of passenger vehicles we saw. There were other Asian manufacturers, but it was extremely rare to see an American made car. After the hills came long stretches of mostly flat grassland ideal for grazing livestock. Sheep and goats herded together while the cattle preferred to be by themselves. Occasionally a herd would decide the grazing was better on the other side of the road. Traffic stopped twice for herds of animals crossing the road.

Just about the time our legs were giving out, we came upon the Nalgar Ger Camp. Olly had made us a reservation there for the night. There was a main central building with a restaurant, surrounded by several gers. A ger is a round tent, usually white, made with a wooden frame covered by canvas. The construction has not changed much in centuries and is brilliantly simple. The round frame is made from what looks like a very large baby gate with struts in a tightly overlapping "X" pattern. When extended, it can form into a circle. A door frame connects both ends. The roof is made by a central ring held up by two long vertical poles. Numerous spokes are inserted into holes along the outer edge of the central ring and secured to the round side wall. Heavy canvases are layered around the outside wall, depending on how much insulation is needed. The same technique is used for the roof. Some gers have flooring made from mats or rolls of linoleum, while permanent gers can have concrete floors. The inside walls are often finished off with decorative tapestries. Nomads put up or take down a ger in under two hours. They tend to get a lot of practice.

We were met by our hosts Antomore and Bimba (not the same one from the bike store) who both really made an effort to make us feel welcome. They showed us our ger and gave us the dinner menu. Thinking we needed protein to repair all the leg muscles we abused, I had mutton (sheep) and Jon had beef, both of which were very delicious. Our ger was quite comfortable with four beds and a bathroom with a shower. After our long day of pedaling, we were glad to be there. The camp sat among vast rolling hills with mountains in the distance. Sheep were grazing on the hills next to the camp. It was a pleasant way to end the first day.

AUGUST 27: BIKING DAY 2 – NALGAR GER CAMP TO MOLTSOG ELS TOURIST CAMP – 28.4 MILES (58.2 BIKING MILES TOTAL)

Breakfast at Nalgar Camp was two fried eggs, toast, and a hot dog. We then loaded up the bikes and headed out. The roads were still busy at times with cars and trucks whizzing by. I appreciated those who smiled or waved because it felt like a little burst of energy. My favorite interactions were the cars with kids who said hello in English. It was obvious that we were not from around there.

That morning, we saw grasslands of gentle rolling hills with occasional herds of livestock. Even herds close to the road would ignore us since the grass was far more interesting than we were. We stopped at a roadside stand where Jon bought a jar of pickles from the woman working there. The stand was a metal framework supporting a green tarp that formed a roof and three walls to provide shade from the sun. Inside were low tables made of plywood and 2x4s with rows of jars containing pickled fruits and vegetables. It was a rare sign of civilization now that we were further from the big city with long stretches of road between the mostly tiny villages.

After we endured a long climb, we stopped at the crest of a hill where there was another tall vertical pole surrounded by a rock base.

Jon at the roadside pickle stand

This was similar but larger than the one we had seen the day before. The base was a pile of rock 15-20 feet wide and 4-5 feet tall, with the central, vertical pole extending another ten feet higher. Unlike the previous one, the top of this pole had support cables running to three outside posts surrounding the base. Strips of cloth (mostly blue, but also white, red, green, and yellow) that were tied to the posts and cables appeared to be the remains of flags left by travelers. There were hundreds of flags all flapping in the constant wind, some so old that the color had nearly faded away. There was a well-worn dirt path around the base in stark contrast to the lush surrounding grassland. Jon and I ate a snack at a small concrete bench nearby, knowing that this site was significant but not sure why.

Shortly after we arrived, an SUV pulled in with a man and four women. The man and three of the women got out to walk around the monument while speaking Mongolian. We said “hello” to the group and one of the women, Nara, answered back in English. She seemed eager to speak with us. I asked her about this place, curious about its significance. She explained that we were standing before a “prayer tower” called an “ovoo” (pronounced owa.) They were usually found atop high hills or along dangerous areas of roadway. Travelers can stop to pray and often leave food or trinkets to ensure a safe journey. The colored cloths were prayer flags placed by previous travelers. The blue flags symbolize the sky, which is considered sacred in Buddhism. While we were talking another car stopped. A family got out and walked around the ovoo tossing rice on it as an offering.

Hilltop ovoo for prayers and offerings to ensure a safe journey

We told Nara about our trip and the final goal of arriving in Ulgii. Nara then took us to their SUV to meet her 92-year-old grandmother, sitting in the front passenger seat. The whole family seemed genuinely thrilled to meet these two strangers on bikes from the United States. We had a great discussion, with Nara translating, about where we were going and the details of our adventure. They seemed excited for us and even posed for a few photos. At that point, the elderly woman stepped out of the SUV and approached me with what looked like rosary beads in her hand. She touched my forehead, closed her eyes, and began speaking in Mongolian. Nara explained she was giving me a blessing for a safe journey. She then did the same for Jon. I felt truly honored to have met this precious family and, of course, for the blessing. This was just the beginning of a long trip which could have many unknown and potential dangers. I was grateful for the beautiful gesture of this sweet woman.

Nara (third from left) and her family, including grandmother (in yellow) who blessed us for a safe journey

After they left the ovoo, we continued on our way. Roughly 25 miles later, we saw a sign for Moltsog Tourist Camp. We turned at the sign and followed the dirt road for several miles. We struggled over the bumpy, rocky, sandy road which required a fair amount of effort. We arrived at the main house, happy to be finished for the day. When we told them we had a reservation, they seemed confused. Assuming it was simply a language issue, Jon gave them the printed reservation receipt while I checked out the available beer selections. A lengthy phone conversation between the Moltsog person and perhaps the manager did not look like a good sign. It turned out there were two Moltsog Tourist Camps. Ours was the other one, further down the road. Disappointed, we got back on our bikes and went down the rocky sand road in the direction she pointed. The problem was, we didn't see another ger camp. After a few miles Jon and I questioned if we could have missed a turn, but there was only one road. Biking on these awful roads was difficult on a good day, but even worse being hot, tired, and carrying 70lbs of gear on a top-heavy bike. I sure was missing that cold beer I did not have a chance to drink. After getting stuck in the sand a few times, we walked our bikes up a large hill. At the top we saw a cluster of gers in the distance. That was the other camp! The added miles were daunting, but we were relieved to have finally found our place to stay.

The camp's main office had the feel of a small hotel lobby. There was an adjoining restaurant decorated with several pictures of Chinggis Khaan on the walls. A dozen or more tables with chairs were ready for patrons, although Jon and I were the only two camp guests.

A short while later we were shown to our ger. The gers were permanent structures with cement floors, clean and surprisingly large with two comfortable beds, one table, and a chair. Beautiful tapestries covered the inside walls. Intricately painted designs were on the furniture and framework of the ger. My only concern was the door being about four feet high. I would be reminded of this every time one of us hit our head on the door frame entering or leaving. Every soft bang followed by a cuss word scored a point. By bedtime the score was tied at two each for the number of times we hit our heads.

Just as we were settling into our ger, there was a knock at the door. A man about 30 years old with jet-black hair, a small black goatee, worn gray pants, and a gray Cannondale biking shirt stood there. The man spoke English well and introduced himself as Houk. He said he and his friend Oora had just cooked dinner and wanted to share it with us. Being tired and hungry, we took them up on their generous offer. We followed Houk to a table shaded by a tarp overhead. Houk explained they had cooked the mutton in a pit, using stones heated in a fire. A large pot had layers of hot stones above and below the seasoned meat. The pot was placed in the fire pit for a couple of hours, allowing the meat to slowly roast.

Houk's wife brought us hot tea along with a platter of mutton that had just been taken out of the hot stones. We did not see the hot stone fire pit, but the meat smelled like it was just taken off a barbeque grill. Jon and I cut off bite size pieces of mutton and devoured them along with pickles and potatoes. The mutton was tender and cooked to perfection. What I initially thought was a crude way to cook produced an elegant result, as good as any fine restaurant.

Oora, probably in his late 40s, was clean shaven and wore a black T-shirt and black baseball-style cap. Oora said (through Houk) that he was the owner of a Japanese restaurant in Ulaanbaatar and another in Canada, where he spends half of the year. We spoke to the two gentlemen for about an hour, and Houk was a wealth of information. He was very interested in our route, and after showing him our maps he made several good suggestions for interesting sites to see, places to sleep, and restaurants along the way. We gladly accepted suggestions from a local.

Houk also spoke about the "peaceful revolution of 1990" when the fall of the Soviet Union created an opportunity for Mongolia to change from Soviet control to an independent democracy. That same year schools stopped teaching the Russian language and instead taught English. That explains why younger people may know some English while older ones do not. Houk also explained the difference between a ger and a yurt. Both terms basically mean the same thing, but "ger" is a Mongolian word while "yurt" is of Russian origin. Most Mongolians prefer to say ger, while in western parts of the country, closer to Kazakhstan, yurt is used more often due to the significant Russian influence over Kazakhstan. I found it interesting that when discussing the Russian invasion of Ukraine, most of the younger Mongolians sided with Ukraine while the older people supported Vladimir Putin and Russia. Houk felt that the Russian influence prior to 1990 was still strong enough for people to align with Russia. Houk was careful to state the facts without bias. At the end, I was not totally sure which side, if any, he supported.

AUGUST 28: BIKING DAY 3 – MOLTSOG ELS TOURIST CAMP TO OLYMPUS HOTEL – 37.7 MILES (95.9 BIKING MILES TOTAL)

The day began with a man trying unsuccessfully to teach me Mongolian. He was about my age, in his 60s, standing by the entrance arch of our tourist camp waiting for his van to arrive. His clothing and hat made me think he could be a tour guide, so I thought I might learn something by speaking to him. He knew a little English, and I only knew a few Mongolian words, but we still had an interesting conversation. I said "san banoo" (the Mongolian word for "hello") to him, and he answered "hello" back. I thought we were off to a good start. I tried a few other Mongolian words I thought I knew. He just smiled that "good try" kind of smile. The word "thank you" in Mongolian is "baa-ru-schlaa" which I struggled to pronounce correctly. We practiced that along with several other words and, as patient as he was, I don't think I earned a passing grade for any of them. The Mongolian Cyrillic alphabet has 35 characters, many of which have sounds not used in English. There are rolling "R's" and "sch" sounds that took me several days to even come close. People seemed to patiently try to understand what I attempted to say, forgiving my poor pronunciation.

After a breakfast of sausage and eggs, Jon and I began our westward biking for the day, pleased that our bike helmets still fit comfortably considering all the lumps on our heads from repeatedly hitting the door frame. We were out in the country now, with plenty of blue sky and sunshine. The dirt, dust, and diesel fumes of the city were no longer a concern. While there was still traffic, most (but not all) drivers slowed down and gave us lots of room. The green rolling hills and flat grassy fields full of grazing animals seemed to go on forever. The asphalt road was mostly a straight line disappearing into the distance. Cattle were common with many standing right at the edge of the road. There was a herd of goats who decided it was a good time to cross the road right as we approached. We arrived just as the last one made it to the other side. I wondered if they even cared about the traffic going by. Maybe watching cars and holding up traffic was their form of amusement.

Throughout the day we saw flat fields spreading for miles with small mountains far in the distance. Small herds of horses roamed freely, and I imagined this was what the old Wild West must have looked like 150 years ago. We were told that all horses were owned by someone, but these had no brands or marks to signify ownership. There were also no gers or people in sight to look after them. Maybe they were free-range wild horses.

We came across a gas station that looked like it had closed years ago. The building reminded me of a 1950s-style gas station, with large plate-glass windows mounted at an angle and an overhang reaching a small island where two gas pumps once stood. Looking through the dirty windows, I could see a dusty counter, empty shelves, and a few boxes. Several pigs were wandering around outside with one lying in a large puddle of mud. Classic!

Several miles later, Jon and I were pleased to find a small mini-mall with a restaurant, coffee shop and restrooms. I didn't know what made them build it there, out in the middle of nowhere, but I was glad they did. It was a great place to stop, rest, and eat. The customers were very friendly and curious about what we were doing. A few people who spoke English carried on wonderful conversations with us.

Another highlight of the day was seeing a group of perhaps a dozen Bactrian camels (two humps!) and a few horses next to some gers. They were about a quarter of a mile off the main road, with a few people standing around them. It looked like a place for tourists to ride camels, but it did not look like they were open for business. It was the first time I had seen a camel outside of a zoo.

It was a long day of biking, and neither Jon nor I had any complaints about legs or butts hurting...yet. I think the padded bike shorts were a wise idea. It was relatively easy biking on the flat sections of road where the miles seemed to fly by. I would occasionally look at my odometer, and it would be six or seven miles further than the last time I looked. It was easy to become mesmerized with the legs on autopilot and the mind soaking in the vast, empty plateau.

We biked as far as seemed reasonable knowing that the next stretch for tomorrow was very rural. We passed the town of Lun which, by Mongolian standards, was a large city with about 2,500 people. We knew of a hotel just outside the city limits. This was to be the last bed and restaurant for the next few days. Olly told Jon about an organic farm run by Sansar, one of his former tour guides. This could be a place to stay tomorrow night, but we had trouble contacting her. Jon used AT&T, I had Verizon and a local SIM card, but we still could not get through to her. The phone service was spotty at best. Fortunately, we were able to contact Olly in Ulaanbaatar who had a way to reach her for us.

The Olympus Hotel outside Lun had a rock-hard bed but the restaurant had cold beer, so it was still better than sleeping in a tent. The wooden bed had a one-inch-thick mat for a "mattress." Since we were the only ones staying in the hotel, we took the liberty of getting extra mats from the other rooms and piled them up on our beds. The rooms were sparse, with two beds, a table, and a chair. One light bulb hung from the ceiling. There were no pictures to hide the torn, dirty wallpaper. Our room with two beds, a communal bathroom on a different floor, and no internet was 100,000 MNT for the night, or about $29 USD. The restaurant wasn't fancy, but it had everything we needed, serving a couple of meat and noodle dishes. Mongolian beer, or "peev," was not bad. We chose local brews, so I had a Borgio and Jon had a Sengur. They tasted like something you would enjoy in a craft brewery.

AUGUST 29: BIKING DAY 4 – OLYMPUS HOTEL TO SANDOR BERRY FARM – 21.8 MILES (117.7 BIKING MILES TOTAL)

Being the only hotel customers, the two women employees reluctantly opened the restaurant just for us. They made each of us a hearty breakfast with three fried eggs, bread, and sausage that reminded me of Taylor's ham (or pork roll, depending on where in New Jersey you live) that my mother used to make when I was a kid. Very tasty!

The biking day began with a steep uphill grade for the first six miles. We struggled to reach the top, only to see the next hill come into view. The brief downhill stretches also involved some work as we tried to gain speed to help us up the next hill. It was frustrating to work so hard up the next hill, only to see a second and a third hill beyond that. I found that the crests of hills were great places to rest, have a snack, and rehydrate. It was a small reward for successfully making it to the top. Some of the hills were so steep that we had to walk the bikes up to the top. Pushing a heavy bike loaded with gear uphill was much slower and burned a lot more energy than riding. There were times when I would take 10-15 steps then need to stop and rest. It was tiring, but I had to remind myself that once we reached the top, there should be a downhill, at least for a little while.

Our mood improved when Jon received a call from Olly. Olly had been in contact with Sansar, his friend at Sandor Berry Farm. The plan was to meet Sansar at km marker 162, where there would be a dirt road that led to the farm. We called Olly when we got close, and again when we arrived at marker 162, but there was no one there to meet us. With only one dirt road to choose from, we took a chance and followed it thinking we would soon meet Sansar.

After a short time, slogging through sand and rock, we decided on a new plan. Sansar lived on a farm, so she must have a truck. There was no need for us to struggle through any more horrible dirt roads. I imagined throwing our bikes in the bed of her fancy, comfortable Ford F-150 and relaxing while she drove us to the farm. We happily unpacked our bikes, knowing we were getting picked up in any minute. Just as we finished unpacking, Sansar's 15-year-old nephew Buyka rode up on his motorcycle and told us to follow him. Jon and I gave each other "the look" saying, without words, that we needed to pack up the bikes again.

We followed Buyka for another 8 km (5 miles) down the rugged dirt road to Sandor Berry Farm. It was difficult to say which is worse for biking, soft sand or steep grades. Both are slow going and not much fun. Everything changed when we arrived at the farm and met Sansar and her family. They warmly welcomed us to their home, which was a beautiful area on a hill with flat land below and mountains in the distance. A small river meandered through it all.

There were three gers surrounding a small cinderblock building containing a dining room and kitchen. Sansar offered us her ger for the night since her husband was away working as a guide for Goyo Travel. The inside of the ger was absolutely beautiful! There were ornate hand-painted designs on the furniture, posts, roof supports, and just about every surface that could be painted. The orange base coat was covered with intricate designs of all colors - gold, blue, green, pink, yellow, black, white - just stunning! In the center was a cast-iron stove which I am sure had lots of action during the sub-freezing winters. Even though it was hot outside, there was a constant cool breeze entering through the door and exiting through the vents in the center of the roof. The walls were covered in detailed tapestries that looked like silk, giving it a regal appearance.

Sansar's ger

We were immediately served lunch consisting of fresh salad, vegetables, and mutton. The dessert was yogurt with raspberry jam. Most of the food was produced on their farm. There was a pitcher of seabuckthorn juice, which tasted like watered-down slightly tart orange juice. It was very good, and I felt a little guilty pouring myself refills from the large pitcher. There was also a bowl of yellow-orange berries, which were seabuckthorn berries. These berries can be eaten raw or used to make juice or jam. Sansar explained that they grow seabuckthorn bushes on their farm and harvest the berries to sell. She offered us a farm tour for later in the day, which we readily accepted. Sansar, who also spoke German, said "sandor" is the German word for seabuckthorn, which was how they named their farm.

Sansar explained that she grew up in a nomadic family, moving from place to place with the changing of the seasons. During the warm summer months, shepherds move their livestock to cooler higher elevations for grazing. Before the cold season arrives, the herd is moved back down to lower elevations to avoid the severe winter weather. Many families have both a summer camp and a winter camp. Even those who are not shepherds may have a second home elsewhere. The life of a nomad is difficult, constantly on the move and unable to truly establish a home base. Sansar said she left that life, going to college in Ulaanbaatar and getting a degree in tourism and hospitality. She used to live and work in the crowded city of Ulaanbaatar as a tour guide for Goyo Travel but missed the freedom of the countryside.

Sansar and her family moved to the farm three years ago to start their business. Because Mongolia is so vast, people can claim a tract of land simply by getting approval from the mayor. After making improvements and living there a few years, the land is yours. Since Mongolians like their space, it is doubtful anyone will claim the land close by. Sansar said her husband built the cinderblock building and installed a well. Having access to a reliable water source was vitally important. She explained the secret to finding water is to look for iris flowers. Where they grow wild, you will find water. There was no public electricity, so everything ran on solar power. Somehow, they had internet, which made the kids very happy. I didn't understand how that worked since the best phone signal was on top of the hill half a mile away. I guess that explained the difficulty we had in calling her.

In the more remote areas of the country, there might be no local schools. The sparse population spread over large distances makes it impractical. Educational opportunities are more widely available in Ulaanbaatar, and boarding schools are a popular option. Sansar's 16-year-old daughter Badmaa was starting at the University in Ulaanbaatar next year, hoping to become a physician. 10-year-old Aagii would soon be going to boarding school in Ulaanbaatar, and their 2-year-old son Bambar was already living with relatives in Ulaanbaatar. At the start of the next school year, all three of her children would be living in Ulaanbaatar. It was only a two-hour drive by car, but when you miss your kids, that is a very long distance.

After lunch, Sansar took us on a hike to visit her neighbors, Sok and Ganii. They lived 2 miles away, over large hills. As we approached their ger, we saw two men with a bucket walking towards several horses. Sansar said they milk mares every two hours and use the milk to make airag. Mare's milk, when fermented, becomes airag, which has been a part of Mongolian culture and hospitality for centuries. I had heard stories about airag and was anxious to try it.

Sok and his son Ganii, invited us into their ger. After entering and circling to the left side, as is customary, we sat on the floor. The new milk was poured into a large plastic drum while Ganii churned it. The fermentation process begins with a starter culture of lactic acid bacteria and yeast. The yeast and bacteria break down the milk carbohydrates, which produce alcohol as a byproduct. It is the same process found in bread, cheese, wine, and beer production.

They had a healthy supply of airag and Sok poured some into a large basin. He then ladled a portion into what looked like a cereal bowl and offered it to me. I knew it was proper to offer and accept things with the right hand, which I did. Not knowing the rest of the proper etiquette, I took a small sip and tried to pass it on. I was politely corrected and told to drink the entire bowl. Sansar took the bowl and drank it all, showing me how to do it. Sok filled the bowl again and handed it to me. Not wanting to disrespect our hosts, I drank the entire bowl this time. It took several sips to drink it all. Airag has an unusual taste, like milk with a touch of club soda. I would say that airag isn't bad, but it isn't good either. I respect the effort that goes into producing it and how popular it is. Let's just say it is an acquired taste.

I handed the bowl back (with my right hand!) to Sok who quickly refilled it. Jon was next to try it, and he successfully completed the same procedure. Ganii and Sok also had their share and were pleased with their brew. Jon later confided that he had the same impression I did. Although they say it is fermented, larger amounts are more stomach upsetting than buzz producing.

Looking around the ger I noticed a collection of medals. Sok and Ganii had won them for horsemanship at the Naadam games, which consisted of the "three manly sports" of horsemanship, archery, and wrestling. Naadam has been going on for centuries, long before the days of Chinggis Khaan in the 13th century and likely started as preparation for warfare. Back in the day, warriors had to ride well, shoot accurately, and be skilled in hand-to-hand combat. Today it is a celebration of Mongolian heritage and traditional nomadic culture. There are scores of smaller local Naadam games throughout Mongolia, which culminate in the large national Naadam Festival every July.

After a second round of airag was passed around, Sok pulled out a small bottle. Sansar explained that Mongolian men carry bottles of snuff, and it is an honor when someone offers it. Snuff is a powdered tobacco product that is a centuries-old tradition. I was aware of snuff being popular among Mongolian men, but I had a dilemma with myself. The pediatrician in me rebelled against tobacco use, and I took pride when I told my young patients that I had never tried any form of tobacco product. I had a discussion in my mind, weighing the downside of tobacco against disrespecting this honorable gesture offered by

Jon's first drink of Airag

these generous people. It was not a long discussion. I took the bottle. The bottle cap had a small spoon and, being a rookie snuff sniffer, I was told to hold my left-hand palm down and place a small amount of snuff on the back of my hand between thumb and index finger. Snuff is the color of tea but finely ground into a powder, like cinnamon or ground nutmeg. They motioned for me to sniff it up my nose, which I did with a cough they found amusing. It caused a nasal tingle and an "opening of the sinuses" kind of sensation. Although it was not necessarily an unpleasant feeling, it was more of a "weirdness" than anything else. Jon took his turn next, and I felt that we were then accepted into Mongolian society.

Next came the third round of airag, and then the fourth. I would have been happy with one small sip but now I was hoping I just could keep it all down. I heard stories of first timers getting sick, and I was hoping that would not be me. Suddenly the door to the ger opened and four adults and a child entered, sat down, and stared at us. They were neighbors who were either curious about the strange visitors or saw that Sok and Ganii were milking horses, which meant fresh airag. Sok poured two more 2-liter size bottles of airag into the basin and shared it with the new arrivals. I was hoping they would drink the airag and forget about us. However, round five of airag found us.

Two hours had passed since we arrived, and it was time to milk the horses again. Mares are milked 8-9 times a day, which produces plenty of airag. This was our cue to leave, and Sok gave us a bumpy ride in the back of his truck back to Sandor Berry Farm. I was very happy that I did not get sick after all that airag and bouncing around!

After dinner of homemade noodles and mutton, salad, and yogurt with raspberry jam, Sansar gave us the farm tour. Jon and I biked three miles to their crop fields, following Sansar and her kids on their motorcycles. I had to wonder why the fields were so far from their home. Sansar said they had planted 2,500 seabuckthorn bushes, and each one was loaded with yellow-orange berries which were handpicked each morning and evening to avoid the midday heat. Life on a farm involved a lot of hard work every day, but at the same time they said it was very rewarding. They looked to be completely self-sufficient. We saw their hen house, which produced 8-9 eggs daily. There were two vegetable greenhouses full of eggplant, broccoli, lettuce, parsley, cucumbers, etc. Mongolia is not known for producing vegetables since the growing season is so short. Greenhouses extend the growing season by two months or more, which allows for an improved harvest. The young cherry and apple trees were expected to produce fruit over the next several years.

It was impressive to see how much had been completed to establish this farm in the few years Sansar and her family had been there. A tremendous amount of work had already been done, but they planned to do more. It took some time to see the entire farm, but it was now dark and we still had to bike the three miles back to our ger. I followed one of the kids on their motorcycle along the moonlit trail, having a general idea of where to go but happy to have a guide.

When we finally made it back, I was looking forward to some sleep. But first, I wanted to tell Val about my day. Being literally half a world away, I had an opportunity every morning and night to call home. I was going to bed as she was waking up. It was a poorly connected WhatsApp call, which dropped a time or two, but it was so good to hear her voice. It was only the fourth day of biking, and I already had some stories to tell.

AUGUST 30: BIKING DAY 5 – SANDOR BERRY FARM TO CHAYDO'S GER – 22.2 MILES (139.9 BIKING MILES TOTAL)

Sansar and Sok agreed to call a friend to arrange a place for us to spend the next night. We were told to meet them at km marker 188 on the main road. After a large breakfast of eggs, pancakes made of fried dough, tea, and seabuckthorn juice, it was time to set out on the dirt road back to the paved road. I felt like we were honored guests as Sansar and her kids all gathered around for hugs and photos as we prepared to leave.

After biking for a mile, we came upon two dirt roads crossing. With four or five miles to go before the main road, we could not determine which was the correct path. There was a ger nearby and I thought it wise to ask for directions. The couple we met spoke no English, but after hand gestures we were directed to one of the trails. After another half mile or so, Sok approached riding his motorcycle. Sok did not speak English either, but motioned for us to follow him. We thought this was a lucky break for him to lead us to the main road. But instead of helping us leave, he led us back to his ger. He again generously offered us some airag. We were grateful for his hospitality, but we would rather have directions to the paved road.

Just then, another motorcycle pulled up. Sansar had come to our rescue. I assume she had been watching us with binoculars. She showed us which trail to take and saved us from any more airag. We thanked both Sok and Sansar for their kindness and we respectfully parted ways. Seven miles later we made it to the paved road, happy to be in civilization again.

It was tough biking in the 80-something degree heat. In the distance we saw what looked like a roadside stand where we might get some cold drinks. When we came closer, we realized it was not a roadside stand but rather someone's house. Jon was curious, and we approached the open door.

A woman invited us in and offered us "oos," meaning water. She and her husband were both around 60 years old. I was sorry I could not get their names. She was busy making lunch while he was taking a nap. I was immediately taken by her friendly eyes. She appeared happy and was very talkative even though neither of us could understand the other. But words did not matter. We appeared to be strangers in need and the right thing to do was to help, giving us what they could from their humble home. The window shades were down, making it dark inside. A cast-iron stove was in the middle of the room next to a chair. On the opposite wall was a sink and counter, making a small kitchenette. Toward the back of the room her husband was lying on the bed.

The one-room house was sparse but appeared to satisfy their needs. She offered us some melon she was in the process of cutting. We took a few bites, enjoying the sweet taste. We then realized they were about to offer us a full lunch. Even people with limited means still give strangers all they can. Not wanting to be a burden or overstay our welcome, we thanked them, made our exit, and moved on down the road.

Just past the 188 km marker there was a man standing next to his car parked off the road. Assuming this was our host, we pulled off the road as he waved to us. He introduced himself as Chaydo and his wife Unga. We followed their car up the dirt road for half a mile or more to their ger. We were taught that when approaching a ger, it was appropriate to yell "hold the dogs" before coming too close. Now I see why. Their three dogs made a lot of noise but were not aggressive since we arrived with Chaydo and Unga. Chaydo yelled "yaw" at the dogs several times and they appeared to understand. It is a great insult to say that to a person, but when directed at a dog it is meant for them to keep quiet and obey. Afterwards the dogs seemed to accept our presence.

Their ger was high on a hill with a great view of the surrounding area and road below. There was a solar panel next to the ger and a large pile of cow dung drying just beyond that. On the other side was a small corral with some calves and Chaydo's horse tied up nearby. We entered their ger and were immediately offered tea and candy. We offered our peanuts and trail mix to them. Chaydo and Unga spoke no English, but their kindness was obvious. Without internet or cell service, my Google translate would not work. Communications were mostly a guess for us all.

Chaydo and Unga's ger was very cozy and contained everything they needed. Gers are circular and seem larger once inside, perhaps 20-25 feet in diameter and tall enough to stand comfortably. The cast-iron stove was in the center with a chimney pipe exiting through the domed roof. Just like other gers we have seen, the furniture and supporting framework was orange with colorful painted designs. To the right of the door was an orange cabinet with ornate decorations painted in blue, white, green, and pink. Next to that was their bed, two beautiful wood carved cabinets, and a bench for seating. The solar panel outside was wired to a car battery on the left side of the door. The battery provided power for a few electrical appliances, like the television and a light. Family pictures and other heirlooms completed the décor. I was impressed by how clean everything was inside their ger. With all the dirt and dung everywhere, the blue linoleum floor was shiny and spotless.

Unga made a mixture of flour and water, then rolled it out flat. Next, she reached into a small metal tub and picked out several pieces of dried dung, placing it into the stove then lighting it with a blow torch. Much to my surprise, it easily caught fire and quickly heated the stove. The rolled flour mixture was placed in a frying pan and a short while later, lunch was served. The rolled flour transformed into a delicious noodle and mutton dish served with tea. I was pleased to learn that neither dried dung nor burning dung produce any odor. I was also happy that Unga washed her hands before making the flour and water mixture, which was finished before handling the dung.

After lunch it was time to tend to our bikes. As I went to unload my bike, I found it lying on the ground. The kickstand had buckled under the extra weight of my backpack and gear. It was bent, like a small leg extending out horizontally from the bike frame. I thought I could make a repair if I had the right tools. I unloaded my bags and took off the kickstand. I showed it to Unga, making a hammering motion with my hand, which she understood and produced a hammer. Chaydo gave me a metal disc to hammer on, which looked like it had come from an old car. I was able to bang it back into shape just enough to hold up the bike, but I knew it could not be trusted to support the full load of gear. Issues were expected to arise, and I thought it would be lucky if this was the biggest problem of the trip. Jon, on the other hand, had problems with his rear derailleur slipping out of first gear going up hills. This was a more significant problem as the hills were only going to get larger. There were three screws on the derailleur, and probably adjusting one of them would fix the problem. But, which one? Since we didn't know, we adjusted all of them just to make sure. Since we didn't make it worse, we thought that was progress.

The afternoon was as hot as Florida but without the humidity. We sat in the shadow of the ger and took in the surroundings. The first thing I noticed was how quiet it was. There were no neighbors, the livestock were grazing somewhere out of view, and the cars and trucks passing by on the distant main road barely made a sound. Every ger had a pile of dung nearby. Dried cow and yak dung were commonly burned for cooking fuel and to keep the ger warm in winter. Without any trees, there was no firewood. We were told the trees had been cut down and used as firewood over the centuries and not replenished. So, Mongolians needed to utilize the resources they had. There was an abundant supply of cow and yak dung, which burned well when dried.

After a dinner of noodles and meat, we spent the rest of the evening watching the milking of the cows. The calves were in a corral, separated from their mothers. The mothers were then secured with a rope. One calf was let out and immediately found his mother to begin feeding. Once the milk flows, the calf was separated, and the cow was milked by Unga. There was a rhythmic squirt sound as the milk hit the bucket. Afterwards, the calf returned to the mother to finish feeding. The process repeated itself as each calf was let out of the corral one by one.

Chaydo then mounted his horse and rode off to round up the other cattle. A short time later, and from seemingly out of nowhere, about 200 cattle magically appeared. I don't know how he found them, much less herding them all back by himself. With Chaydo's return, Unga motioned it was time to drink. She had boiled the fresh cow's milk, allowed it to cool, then served it. The milk was very good, lighter than I expected and with a unique taste unlike any other milk I had ever tried.

At bedtime, Chaydo and Unga cleared a large area for us on the floor. Their bed was on the right side of the ger, and we had floor space on the left. Our hosts seemed impressed with our air mattresses. We were provided with quilts for our bedding, and they made things as comfortable as possible. The language barrier was not a huge problem, although it did lead to some slightly awkward situations. We did not want to interrupt their normal routine, but we had no way to know what time they went to sleep. I was sure they were being polite in allowing us to do what we wanted, and we were trying to follow their cues as to when to lay down. They would smile at us, we would smile at them, and neither of us wanted to exert undue influence on the other.

Our plan for the next day was to find a hotel in Erdenesant, which we thought was about 30 km (19 miles) away. This fell short of our 50 km daily goal, but we agreed to be flexible with our itinerary. We were prepared for camping, but if beds, warm showers, and restaurants were available, we didn't mind a few comforts. Staying here and at Sandor Berry Farm the night before weren't planned but the experiences were priceless.

AUGUST 31: BIKING DAY 6 – CHAYDO'S GER TO ERDENESANT – 20.8 MILES (160.7 BIKING MILES TOTAL)

Morning began early with the sound of mooing and another milking of the cows. The milking process of last evening repeated itself. Chaydo tended to the cows while Unga prepared breakfast. There was fresh cow's milk from the morning milking, along with rice soup, tea, and a platter of bones with two sharp knives to cut off pieces of meat. Unga had boiled sheep bones and used the broth for the rice soup. Nothing goes to waste, since their survival depends on it. When Chaydo finished with the cows, we all ate breakfast.

After breakfast, Chaydo dressed in a fine blue riding coat that extended down the length of his legs. He had a gold sash for a belt, which, along with black boots, appeared quite formal. As we were preparing our bikes, we said goodbye to him as he rode off toward his herd of cattle. When the bikes were ready, we each paid Unga 70,000 MNT (just over $20 USD) for their hospitality, which was the prearranged amount. $20 for a night's lodging, three meals, and an amazing experience seemed like a bargain. Overall, five-star hosts.

We rode about 20 miles to Erdenesant over mostly flat, paved roads. These were the types of roads that made it easy to cover long distances quickly. About halfway, there was a large oovo where we stopped for a short break and a snack in the shade. A monument in a fenced area caught our eye as we entered through a gate. There were five life sized statues of a camel, sheep, cow, goat, and horse all standing side by side on a large horizontal pedestal. Above them was a sign reading "100" held up by two metal posts resembling wheat stalks. Below was a word written in large red Cyrillic letters that I understood to be "Erdenesant." The town of Erdenesant was established in 1920, so I thought the statues must commemorate their centennial. There were three plaques but, since Google translate was not working, I could not understand them. One plaque had a Cyrillic title stating something about Erdenesant, with musical notes and what looked like song lyrics. I could only guess about the details.

Staying there for the night made for a short low-mileage day but, since the next town was another 50-55 km away, it made sense. With our maps showing no sign of civilization between here and the next town, we both thought the smart thing was to call it a day! We were always willing to adjust our plans for assurances of food and hotels if we could find them. We were there for the experience, not to abuse ourselves.

Erdenesant was off the main road, about 4 km down a dirt road. The town was a cluster of homes with a few buildings, the tallest being four stories. I suppose we were staying in the "suburbs," about 2 km beyond the road to town. There were a small group of stores and four restaurants along the main road. We picked one of the restaurants that reminded me of a "Mom and Pop" type of place – the kind I thought would have "good home cooking." We ate a filling lunch of rice, meat, vegetables with meat soup, and a dumpling. I believed we picked the right place, and just in time, as a tour bus soon arrived with 20 or more tourists that filled the small room.

After discussing our options, or lack thereof, we decided that tents would be our choice for the night. There was a hotel in Erdenesant but staying there would have meant backtracking about 6 km each way over dirt roads. Since the restaurant was nearby, we did not feel biking the extra distance was worth it. We made our camp a little over half a mile from the main road, next to a small sports arena that looked like a Little League baseball field without a marked infield.

Later that afternoon we noticed a growing number of people and horses gathering outside the arena. Eventually dozens of horses with their young riders wearing numbered vests began to trot down the well-worn dirt path away from the arena. Everyone followed, as we did, to a white line across the path which appeared to be a finish line. The riders disappeared down the path, over a hill, and out of sight, towards a distant starting point. The spectators appeared to be having their version of a tailgate party, like you would see before a college football game. A young girl approached us with a basket and offered us homemade snacks followed by a gentleman handing us two cups of airag.

This was clearly a youth and family event, with the older generation in more traditional Mongolian dress - colorful riding coats with cloth sashes for belts - and the younger generation wearing Air Jordan/ Chicago Bulls T-shirts with New York Yankees hats. I wondered if they knew the meaning of the emblems, or even the teams they represented, but I felt a touch of home and was thankful they considered them interesting. It seemed like I had seen either a Bulls or Yankees logo at least once every day.

A short time later we saw a small cloud of dust on the hill, then a rider appeared, followed by two or three more. This became a line of riders coming in fast at full gallop, trying to jockey for position. As they came by, I noticed the riders were around 6-12 years of age. They were greeted at the finish line by their smiling families as they dismounted from their horses. Mongolians take pride in their horsemanship, carrying on the traditions of Chinggis Khaan over the centuries. I assumed these local events were training for the regional Naadam Games, leading to the annual National Naadam Festival in mid-July.

SEPTEMBER 1: BIKING DAY 7 – ERDENESANT TO BICHIGT KHAD TOURIST CAMP – 35.5 MILES (196.2 BIKING MILES TOTAL)

After camping in tents that night, I must say it was not the best night of sleep I ever had. There was just enough road noise to keep me awake even though we were almost a mile away. There were other noises throughout the night, perhaps cows, along with barking dogs somewhere in the distance. The ground felt hard even with the air mattress. It was supposed to be 50 degrees, so instead of my 20-degree sleeping bag, I just used the fleece liner. I was a little cold at about 3 a.m. but not cold enough to get in my sleeping bag. Jon and I both woke up around 6 a.m. to a beautiful sunrise over the mountain. I had a breakfast of tea, Russian oatmeal, and a yogurt cup, which came from the food stored in my pannier bags. We knew we had a thirty-mile day, so we started out around 8:30 down the road.

The roads were paved and in pretty good shape. I knew a bike lane was too much to ask for, but I wished for it anyway. There was a sweet spot at the far right of the pavement – too far right puts you in the dirt and gravel shoulder, while too far left puts you in the way of traffic, which by now was just a few cars an hour. There were occasional potholes but not as many as there are in Tennessee. I thought the Tennessee Department of Transportation should come to Mongolia to learn how to deal with their pothole problem. Still, I knew to stay vigilant. Hitting one good pothole could throw me off the bike, bend a wheel rim, or cause some other trip-ending disaster. I enjoyed the scenery immensely but also kept an eye on the road.

We made good time without encountering any significant hills. We also did not encounter many signs of civilization. It was mostly flat, wide-open space dotted with grazing sheep, goats, and cattle. Seeing a small herd of camels was always worth stopping for a photo opportunity.

Eventually we came upon Ulaanshiveet, a town which looked like it had grown in size since our satellite map image was taken. We stopped for a short break to decide whether to have lunch now or at the tourist

Sheep and goats grazing together

camp 10 km away, where we planned to spend the night. Just then, a man hailed us in English and said there was food and a place to sleep just ahead. He came over and introduced himself with a long, complicated sounding name that neither Jon nor I could remember. He asked if we were Americans, saying he liked America. We commented on how well he spoke English, and he explained he had lived in the United States for ten years, mostly in New York, Washington, and San Francisco. We showed him our maps and asked about the Bichigt Khad Tourist Camp. He said it was only 2 km away, or maybe 3 km at the most. He confirmed there were restaurants, showers, and places there to spend the night. I was pleased to hear it was much closer than we thought. The end of the day meant food and a (hopefully) comfortable bed. We thanked him for the good news, took some selfies, and biked on with renewed energy. We went 3 km, then 4 and 5 km, with no sign of the tourist camp. Tired as we were, we knew it was out there somewhere, so we biked on. After almost 9 km, buildings and gers began to appear in the distance. Our estimation of 10 km from Ulaanshiveet turned out to be correct as Jon's satellite maps were very accurate.

I expected a small ger camp but instead found the "Buc-ee's" of Mongolia. The Khaan Buuz looked like a small shopping mall with restaurants (including one Japanese), coffee shops, a market, and restrooms. It looked like a regular stop for tourists considering the number of long-distance motorcoach buses in the parking lot.

The Bichigt Khad Tourist Camp next door offered gers for 200,000 MNT a night (about $58) and cabins for 300,000 MNT a night (about $87). The gers were permanent, conical, teepee-like structures made of cement with skylights and a protruding front door. Behind them were unusual formations of large boulders unlike anything I had seen previously in Mongolia. It reminded me of something you would see in the canyons of Utah. There were small trees growing in the rock, the first natural trees I had seen so far. It had a definitive southwest US feeling. We thought we deserved the upgrade after sleeping in tents last night, so for about $40 each we opted for the cabin. The one-room cabin had two small beds, two large beds, a table, and a front porch with a table and chairs. It was a short walk to the Water Closet, or bathhouse, with showers shared by the entire tourist camp.

We unloaded our gear and headed to the Japanese restaurant. We both chose meatballs, rice, mashed potatoes, shredded cabbage, and carrots, all for 14,000 MNT ($4 USD) each. The menus were written in Mongolian with photos of the dishes, and this one looked like a hearty meal for a hungry biker. I also had rice tea, which looked like iced tea but had a distinctive rice flavor. It was actually quite tasty.

Adjacent to the restaurant was a small market with food items and a few other basic essentials. I picked out a drink and a snack for later, then made my way to the check out. A young woman in her early 20s, with dark hair and a business-like attitude, was at the cash register, along with her young child playing behind the counter. She totaled the purchase and pointed to the screen that said 7,500 MNT. I took out my wallet and handed her a 20,000 MNT bill. She took the money, then pointed to the screen again showing 7,500 MNT. I said to take it out of the money I gave her, but she did not speak English and just pointed to the screen. Assuming she needed exact change, I dug through my wallet and came up with the 7,500 MNT. She took the money, nodded, and smiled. I asked her for the 20,000 MNT bill back and was given the "I don't know what you are talking about" look. I didn't know if she understood English, but when I said "I just gave you 20,000 MNT" she acted clueless. Being a busy place popular with tourists, there happened to be a tour guide in line behind me who could translate. I told him what happened, and he had a conversation with her. He told me she did not know anything about that, and I must be a confused tourist. When I protested, he said there was a video surveillance camera the manager could review. I thought "Great, that will prove what I am saying."

At this point, those two annoying voices of right and wrong popped up on my shoulders. The devil said "If she is scamming you, she is scamming others as well. This side hustle of cheating tourists is not right. The video will prove it!" The angel said "This poor woman probably does not make much money, and she has a young child to support. Do you really want to cause problems, and maybe get her fired, all over $6 USD?" Rationalization can be a powerful tool at times. I told her, through the interpreter, that she could keep the money but to please use it for her child. If she needed six dollars that much, she was welcome to it.

The walk back to our cabin was a short one. We needed to do laundry, and the community Water Closet had sinks large enough to rinse out clothes. The low humidity made for quick drying. A shower was next on the list. While doing laundry, a young man employed by the tourist camp came in and handed me a towel with small packets of body gel and shampoo. I thanked him as he quickly left. I wondered if he was trying to tell me something...

The soft beds were inviting, and a nap seemed in order after our long day of biking. Having done laundry and taken a shower, my chores were complete. Ninety minutes later, I woke up refreshed. I wrote a blog two days earlier but could not post it until I found reliable Wi-Fi. The internet connection was strong here, so I wrote another blog and posted them both. This also meant I could make calls on WhatsApp to my wife, daughter, son, and father-in-law to cap off the evening. A good Wi-Fi connection was a real treat! Sure, I was having a cool adventure, but there is nothing better than talking to family halfway around the world. I enjoyed hearing news from home since we were completely cut off from any real media. I found sports and politics to be the news items of most interest. It was a relief to be away from the constant political fighting, but in an odd way I was still curious about it. More importantly, I was longing for news about college football. Being Sunday morning in Mongolia, I wanted to know about yesterday's Florida State University football game. Being Saturday evening at home, they often had not finished the game yet. The 13-hour time difference meant my morning was beginning as their previous day was ending. Above all else, just hearing the voices of my family helped to lessen the distance between us. I realized how easy it was to take for granted that my wife lives in the same home that I do and could see her every day. Now it has been a couple of weeks since I last saw her, and it will be several more weeks until I do again. I missed having her by my side. Hearing her voice was always comforting.

SEPTEMBER 2: BIKING DAY 8 – BICHIGT KHAD TOURIST CAMP TO THE ELEPHANT – 32.8 MILES (229.0 BIKING MILES TOTAL)

We woke up in our cozy little cabin knowing that today was going to be a big biking day. This would be a long stretch of rural countryside, so we had no specific goal for a place to be at the end of the day. There was likely going to be a lot of tent camping in our future, so we thought we would enjoy a good restaurant breakfast then hit the road.

We went to the Japanese restaurant but found there was no power. In fact, the entire complex had no power. I then heard the sound of a generator. I was quite familiar with this sound, having lived on the Florida Gulf Coast for over 30 years, suffering through numerous tropical storms, hurricanes, and power outages. We were told they were able to cook a limited breakfast, for which we were grateful. Soon we enjoyed a hearty breakfast of eggs, toast, and hot dogs.

Packing the bikes did not take too long, although Jon might have had a different opinion on that. He put his bags in his trailer and was ready to go. I had to secure my backpack to the cargo rack, then tie down the equipment bag on top of that. After a bit of trial and error, I found a specific way to tie it all down and prevent things from shifting. A little extra time now will save me from repacking it later if it were to spill out all over the road. Jon was always kind about patiently waiting for me. At least he never said anything about it.

A short way from Bichigt Khad we came to Bayan Gobi, or "Little Gobi," a large area with sand dunes like the Gobi Desert which was to the south of us. We did not plan to go near the Gobi, but many people do take tourist trips there. It is a vast, sandy desert that straddles the border of Mongolia and China. These sand dunes before us looked a bit out of place sandwiched between grass plains and mountains.

Camel rides were a popular attraction, and we saw a group of camels standing near a cluster of four gers. Bactrian (two hump) camels are native to central Asia and the Gobi Desert. Fat is stored in the humps, which may be used for nutrition when needed. There was a small blanket spread between the humps which looked like an improvised saddle. The ornately painted doors of the gers were open, but I only saw two people, and it did not look like they were ready for business. I was tempted to take a camel ride if they were.

We had been following the same road since leaving Ulaanbaatar, which greatly helped reduce our chances of getting lost. Now it was time to make an all-important right turn on Kharkhorin Road, which conveniently led to Kharkhorin, a large town with a hotel. It was a two-day bike trip with no towns along the way. I made sure to check my water and food supply before leaving Bichigt Khad. I could carry eight liters of water, and it only took about fifteen minutes to filter enough to top it off. I had far more food and water than I needed for two days, but planning for the unexpected was always a wise idea. Jon and I were self-sufficient with tents, camp stoves, and supplies. Entering the more desolate stretches of countryside made us even more cautious. We could handle the usual problems but tried to anticipate and prevent any trip ending disasters!

Road sign showing Kharkhorin 52 km away

The road was more uphill than down, but there was less traffic which allowed us to relax a bit and enjoy the ride. We saw long stretches of countryside, with the only sound being the soft roar of my tires on the pavement, the gentle breeze of air through the bike helmet, and the chirping of crickets in stereo from both sides of the road. It was a nice change from the crazy city traffic experienced a week ago. On a hilltop was a small group of white buildings. It was probably a monastery, but being far away and without a road to get there, it was not worth investigating.

Jon's map had a landmark about halfway to Kharkhorin simply marked "elephant." We did not yet understand the significance of the elephant because, as far as we knew, elephants were not native to Mongolia. After cycling for most of the day, we were excited to see a stone elephant statue in a fenced enclosure just off the side of the road. Also in the enclosure was a banyan tree, a fruit bearing tree important to Buddhists. Associated with Buddha's enlightenment, the banyan tree symbolizes wisdom, growth, and locations for offerings, reflection, and meditation. The canopy provides shelter, and the extensive root system symbolizes the interconnectedness of all living beings. Since it was hot, we decided to sit under the only shade tree we found so far in Mongolia. This, we thought, would be a good place to camp for the night. Being quiet and out of the way, we set up our tents and made our campsite.

The elephant was about six feet tall and stood on a two-foot-tall pedestal. On its back was a bird, sitting on a rabbit, sitting on a monkey, which sat on the elephant. My understanding is that in Buddhism, this depicts the "four harmonious friends," with the bird (sky), rabbit (underground), monkey (tree), and elephant (ground) all representing the terrestrial habitats. I have also come across a more existential interpretation where the bird (soul), rabbit (emotions), monkey (wandering mind), and elephant (physical body) relate to the human condition. I do not know if one or both interpretations are correct and may need to discuss this with a Buddhist philosopher.

The "Elephant," our campsite for the night

The elephant was more popular than we anticipated, as several cars stopped to see this unique statue. We welcomed the visitors to our campsite as they welcomed us to their significant site. One visitor gave us each a cookie as we talked about our bikes. He was Asian, young and fit, who said he was a professional biker. He was quite interested in our trip, which gave me the impression he would like to try it someday. Later on, a car pulled up with a man who appeared to be Korean. Neither of us spoke the other's language, so we mostly smiled and nodded our heads. He went to his car and returned with two pinecones, giving one to each of us. We must have looked a little confused, not knowing what to do. He then gave us that "Seriously?" look and proceeded to show us how to peel the pinecone to expose the edible pine nuts within. My wife and I occasionally cook with pine nuts at home, but we get them in a bag from the store. I guess I should have realized there is a step or two before they get in the bag, but I never thought about it.

In the distance we saw black clouds forming with the soft rumble of thunder. What luck, I thought, caught in a thunderstorm under the one tree in sight. Eventually the rain came, just a few drops, then stopped. It was a good thing we did not have to move our tents since the storm was so brief. I would have hated to be hit by a bolt of lightning because we were under the only tree!

Dinner in camp involved eating our packaged food heated by a small isobutane camp stove. My creation that night was pasta, tuna, and a tomato-pepper sauce from a pouch written in Russian that might have been ketchup. Most of our food came from the "Hypermarket" in Ulaanbaatar. It reminded me of the gourmet dinners we made in the college dorm with a hot pot.

Finally, as the sun began to set and after the human visitors departed, the grazing sheep and horses began to stroll by for a visit. Our tents were inside the fenced area with the elephant statue, so we felt safe from nighttime visitors - except for the field mice that were everywhere. We had seen evidence of them in many places, but this was the first time we saw them up close. They were kind of cute when they poked their heads up from their burrows and ran around briefly before disappearing down another burrow. It looked like a giant game of "Whack-A-Mole." I was concerned they might get into our food bags, so we placed them high on the fence which kept our food out of their reach.

As the evening ended, we were surrounded by a flock of birds sitting on the fence and in the tree. Since this was the only tree in sight, they must visit frequently. There might have been a hundred of them, all singing a relaxing song. The symphony of random chirps blended into a harmonious melody lasting over an hour. It only ended when the sunlight had sufficiently faded, and the night began.

SEPTEMBER 3: BIKING DAY 9 - THE ELEPHANT TO KHARKHORIN – 26.2 MILES (255.2 BIKING MILES TOTAL)

Last night we were both tired and out of Wi-Fi range, so early bed seemed like a good idea. The birds eventually quieted down but we were not far off the road, so traffic noise continued into the night. Then came the horses. Their clomping hooves around our safe, fenced area sounded like they were coming right into my tent. I never realized how often a horse snorts. Sometime in the middle of the night, my air mattress became unplugged and went flat. It wasn't too bad considering my soft sleeping bag and the thick grass under the tent provided some cushion. But I liked the added comfort from my air mattress.

The birds awakened us promptly at sunrise, about 6 a.m. Their pleasant chirping last evening turned into an unwanted early alarm clock. As we were making breakfast, a car pulled up with a Mongolian driver/guide and two women tourists to see the elephant. They opened the gate of our little fenced campsite and entered. One woman was from South Korea but lived in Belgium, and the other was from Russia. Both were probably in their late 20s. I resisted the urge to talk politics with the Russian woman. I was very curious about her thoughts on the current war in Ukraine. It might have been an interesting conversation, but probably impolite to bring it up. Instead, she spoke fondly of the friendly people and interesting sights from several visits to the US. We mostly spoke about our families, homes, and Mongolian travel adventures. They were on a small private car tour, and we were two fools crossing the country on bicycles. Even though we were all from different countries and backgrounds, each of us had more in common than not. We listened to and respected each other as fellow travelers in an interesting land. It was an enjoyable conversation and, as they drove away, we waved and wished each other well. I felt a little like a "goodwill ambassador" for our country. I thought about how important it is for people to relate to one another. It seems a shame that politics can get in the way of people being friends.

We cycled along until midday, mostly uphill, until we came to rest on the crest of a small ridge. A car pulled up behind us and a man got out dressed in full Mongolian fashion. He wore a long brown riding coat with a gold sash for a belt. He showed interest in our bikes and agreed to have a picture taken with me. Conversations were a challenge with the language barrier. There were a lot of hand gestures with smiling and nodding. We explained we were going to Kharkhorin, and Jon showed him the map. He understood, nodding his head. We soon waved goodbye and continued on our way.

Next, we passed a herd of 15-20 wild horses standing by the side of the road. They all looked strong and well fed. We briefly interrupted their grazing as they watched us ride by. They did not seem bothered when I stopped to take a few pictures of them. It seemed like their lives were fairly predictable and I wondered if they could even conceive of the oddity we were from halfway around the world.

Several miles later we were passed by ten identical black numbered SUVs, all from the same tour group. It looked like one of those Secret Service presidential convoys going by. We caught up with them a short time later at a restaurant/coffee shop/restroom stop along the road. Their group packed the restaurant, and as we waited in line several came over to talk to us. They were well-dressed millennials, compared to us being sweaty old guys. In perfect English, they said they were part of a large group from Singapore on a motorcoach tour through Mongolia. They seemed interested in our biking trip, asking many questions. They thought it was bizarre that we would bike all that distance. Maybe they were right.

We had a wonderful conversation in languages neither of us understood

Our goal for the day was to reach the Ikh Khorum Hotel in Kharkhorin. We had been told it was a luxury hotel, and after camping out and sweating all day, "luxury" sounded like a great word. We eventually arrived at the Ikh Khorum which, indeed, was very nice. There was a wide lobby with white marble floors, a restaurant, plenty of guest rooms with soft beds, and actual showers with hot water! This was definitely better than camping out in tents. After the bikes were stored in their garage, I walked around the grounds past the gardens in a courtyard. The plants added a nice touch of color. The flashes of red, yellow, white, and green flowers showed beauty and tranquility. Towards the back of the property a new building was under construction for additional hotel rooms. In the larger cities, like Kharkhorin, it was not uncommon to see construction cranes and new buildings halfway completed. What I did not see very often was actual work being done. It made me think of the orange barrels on our roads at home that seem to stay there for years for no apparent reason!

Kharkhorin (also spelled Kharakhorum) was founded by Chinggis Khaan in 1220. At its peak, it was one of the largest cities in the world and capital of a Mongol empire that stretched from modern day eastern Europe to the Sea of Japan, encompassing most of China and large parts of Russia. It was kind of mind blowing to think that hundreds of years ago Chinggis Khaan walked on this same ground. Kharkhorin is still an important city, although with a population of approximately 15,000 it is much smaller than it was centuries ago.

Only 1 km away from the hotel was the Erdene Zuu Monastery. Thought to be the oldest Buddhist monastery in Mongolia, it dates to at least 1585, and some think it may have originated as far back as the 8th century. We walked through an impressive three-story gated entryway into the main compound. It was a huge complex which could easily fit 3 or 4 football fields within its high perimeter brick walls surrounding the centuries-old buildings. I counted 14 temples, either one or two levels tall. Most of them were red with green high-pitched roofs. The area around the entry doors had intricate designs brightly painted with multiple colors in exquisite detail.

Erdene Zuu is still an active monastery, and as we approached one of the temples, we could hear the soft, low chanting of monks. They were in a small red brick temple building with decorative green banding at the top. The roof was made of green terracotta tile, inlaid with a colorful diamond pattern of red and yellow. The eaves of the roof swept out from the center to form an overhang. Some roofs were layered, as you would see in a pagoda. Upon entering, we saw the monks dressed in colorful robes facing each other, seated on opposing benches while chanting in unison. Their low baritone voices combined into one musical chant. They ignored the tourists watching them, which I guessed was not uncommon for them. Unfortunately, no photos were allowed and, even though I thought about sneaking one, I did not want to disrespect this holy place. There was a reverent vibe here given its history of peace, destruction, and rebuilding over the centuries.

We visited several other temples within the monastery compound, meeting Buddha statues of all sizes that stared back at us. Beautiful tapestries and painted murals covered every inch of the walls. The ceilings were hand painted centuries ago and still showed vibrant, bright colors. The attention to detail was amazing, with tiny, thin eyebrows and facial expressions that seemed to come alive. My admiration of these ancient relics left me with a recognition of something larger than myself.

A map of the monastery compound showed that one of the temples was dedicated to the Dalai Lama. The title "Dalai Lama" is given to the spiritual leader of Buddhists throughout Tibet, Nepal, Mongolia, and adjacent lands. I asked if the current Dalai Lama had ever visited the monastery, and no one knew. Jon brought photos of the Dalai Lama to give to friends we met along the way. Revered for his compassionate, nonviolent teachings, they were always graciously accepted.

The Erdene Zuu Monastery is called "the land of 1,000 Buddhas." There were many Buddha statues of all sizes, and each one had a significant meaning. Some are protectors, some represent the sun or moon, and others represent paradise, medicine, or other Buddhist virtues. I

Erdene Zuu Monastery

Buddha statues inside a temple

have observed that Buddhists seem to be very kind and peaceful, with "service to others" being a primary tenet. Compassion and wisdom are essential to Buddhism. They believe in "karma," meaning that actions have consequences. I would think these beliefs are universal truths and should be common to all. Buddhism is the world's 4th largest religion. Mongolia primarily practices Tibetan Buddhism, which is not just a religion but a philosophy of life.

After visiting this amazing holy place, I found it difficult to understand how anyone could feel threatened by Buddhism. How could Stalin attempt to destroy Buddhism by bombing temples and murdering monks? What a tragedy, and a loss for all the world. Fortunately, some temples, like this one, survived. I think we all have a lot to learn, and the ideas taught here can benefit everyone, both Buddhists and non-Buddhists alike.

Reflecting on our day while walking back to the Ikh Khorum Hotel, we came upon a small pizza place. We thought pizza and beer would be a nice change from mutton and noodles, so we stopped in. The menu was very limited, not exactly what we thought, but the beer was good. We returned to the hotel restaurant for some real food. The hotel had one of the best restaurants in town. The menu had a good variety with a few items other than noodles and meat, and the food was delicious. I had a scrumptious meal for around $8 USD. We ended our day with good food, hot showers, and comfortable beds. Who could ask for anything more?

SEPTEMBER 4: BIKING DAY 10 - KHARKHORIN TO A FIELD SOMEWHERE BETWEEN KHOTONT AND ALTAN-OVOO – 34.9 MILES (290.1 BIKING MILES TOTAL)

I enjoyed my stay at the Ikh Khorum Hotel and felt a little sad to leave. As I was packing my bike after breakfast, a man and woman traveling by motorcycle noticed me in the parking lot. The man came over and started a brief conversation. He was Portuguese and the woman was Russian. It was fascinating to speak with people from all over the world. I told him our final goal was Ulgii. He said they started in Ulgii, crossed the Gobi Desert, and were traveling to Ulaanbaatar. From there they planned to take the train to Russia. I had assumed, incorrectly I guess, that travel to and from Russia might be difficult with the current war in Ukraine. Maybe since he was not a Russian citizen it would be easier. I just knew we planned to stay far away from the Russian border.

The biking was mostly uphill. The farther west we went, the higher the mountain peaks. We had not even reached the big mountains yet, but it was still tough going uphill with 60-70lbs of gear on my bike. Just when I climbed to the top of one hill, the next one came into sight. And guess what? After that hill was another hill. I knew the upgraded bike seat and padded biking shorts were good investments to prevent saddle soreness. Unfortunately, I didn't have anything to help my thighs other than Ibuprofen. The morning stiffness usually resolved in the first half mile, and I felt fine until I hit those steeper grades. That was when I felt the "thigh burn."

We came upon an area with a log cabin style building and corrugated metal roof next to a few gers. The sign on the building was written in Mongolian except for "Coca-Cola" on the bottom. I was hoping to buy a snack but could not find any people. The only life I saw were horses grazing a few yards away. After settling for the snacks in our bags, we pushed on. We occasionally passed gas stations along the road. I was disappointed to discover that gas stations only sell gas and oil. That's it, just gas and oil. No mini-mart, no snacks, no cold drinks, and, worst of all, no restrooms. Formal public restrooms are nonexistent in many areas of Mongolia. We have seen cars pulling off the road and the occupants running a few yards away to relieve themselves. In more populated areas outhouses were considered an advancement. I hope they remembered their toilet paper!

We rode through the town of Khotont at midday and decided to find shade and eat lunch while we escaped the heat. We found a small market well-stocked with anything we could want but settled for a cold fruit drink and a banana. We sat in the shade of a building across the street from the market enjoying our fruity dessert. Being another hot day, it was great to rest and cool off for a short while.

Khotont is large enough to be on a map yet small enough to have only one paved road, with just a few businesses on each side. The dirt roads lead up the hill to where the locals live. Being curious, I looked up the population of Khotont which in 2021 was around 4,400 people. That surprised me, thinking it would be more like several hundred, but I assumed the published number was accurate. I had to wonder where all the people were. The small businesses along the road would employ a few, but nowhere near 4,400. There is not another town close enough for a commute. I doubt they are all at home working online!

Knowing that the next town (Altan-Ovoo) would be too far to go in one day, we rode until the combination of sun and fatigue made us stop. With wide open land everywhere, we found an area with several posts just off the road that could have been a corral at one time. There were two gers higher up in the hills and this may have been grazing land for their livestock. With no animals in sight, we decided to make camp.

The first order of business was to create shade. Exposure to constant heat and sun became oppressive after a while. Jon took the tarp from his tent, and we tied it between two posts to block the sun. We set up our camp chairs in the shade and enjoyed the nice breeze. Jon and I sat facing the road observing the desolate landscape. It made me think of a recent trip that Val and I had to a dude ranch in Tucson, Arizona. The dry, hot, Mongolian landscape with scrub vegetation and hard sandy soil had a certain beauty but was also a difficult place to survive. The only vegetation was short grass that I thought was even too little for sheep and goats to graze. At least Arizona had cactus. After a brief rest, we set up our tents and organized our gear. I tried to take a nap but that was difficult in the heat. At least we both had some time to rest.

As Jon and I checked our maps and discussed plans for the next couple of days, a motorcycle pulled up and stopped. A very cheerful man got off and rambled to us in Mongolian even though we let him know we did not understand. He spoke no English, but we figured out his name was Baatiglee. He looked about 40 years old, a little overweight, and likely had been outside working all day in his blue T-shirt, black pants, and well-worn boots. The small blue cap did little to protect his rosy cheeks from the sun. He used the word "Anglo" which I had heard before and meant American. We nodded yes, and that was about all we understood using language. He pointed to the two gers about a mile away which we understood was his home. He motioned "food" and "sleep" to us which we took as an invitation. We agreed to come with him, riding our bikes behind his motorcycle.

He warmly welcomed us to his humble ger and gave us two stools to sit on. The ger was sparse but comfortable. There were three beds, but it appeared he lived alone. He proudly showed us photos that we assumed to be family. My understanding was they were his parents, wife, and children. He also pointed to the medals he won for his horsemanship. I proudly showed him a picture of my wife riding a horse when we were in Tucson, which made him smile. He apparently had been in the military and, if I understood him correctly, was a wrestler.

Baatiglee took out two cups, carefully cleaned them with what might have been a clean rag, and poured each of us a cup of tea. He then offered us a small bowl of hard white pieces of what looked like tile, but we believed it was cheese. He motioned for us to eat, but it was as hard as a brick. There was no taking a bite for fear of breaking a tooth. We politely tried to nibble on the cheese as he opened a drawer and pulled out some wafer cookies, which were quite good. He then left, going to the other ger, and returning with a loaf of bread. Baatiglee cut some pieces, spread butter on the bread and poured sugar on top. That was also very tasty.

Next, he excitedly showed off his short-wave radio and small television. He turned on the TV to a news station showing a woman speaking in either Mongolian or Russian. I couldn't tell the difference. Like most gers, this was all powered with a car battery charged by a solar

Our good friend and generous host Baatiglee

panel. To watch TV, simply connect the wires from the TV directly to the car battery. The entire time he spoke in Mongolian as if we could understand him. Even though we returned dumb blank stares, he continued to talk anyway. It did not seem to matter that we understood nothing he said. He probably did not get many visitors and was happy to have some company.

Baatiglee then pulled out a small snuff bottle. We knew this was quite an honor, so of course we had to accept. I scooped up a tiny amount of snuff and placed it on the back of my left hand. Again, I struggled briefly with my aversion to tobacco, but I couldn't insult our host by refusing. I sniffed it up my nose, which gave Baatiglee a big smile. The tingling sensation swept through my nose and sinuses. I came to the same conclusion as before – snuff is neither pleasant nor unpleasant, but not worth doing when I get home. Jon was next, doing the same and pleasing our host.

The final offering was a clear liquid poured from a small metal pot into a bowl. Baatiglee motioned that we could dip our hard cheese into it, which we did, but that did nothing to soften it. He then motioned for us to drink. I trusted Baatiglee was offering us something special, so I took a small sip. It reminded me of airag but being colorless, I was not exactly sure what it was. I assumed it was some kind of homemade alcohol. He then took out a small, plastic Coca-Cola bottle. Leaving the ger briefly, I could see him washing out the bottle. He returned, carefully dried it with a rag, then filled the bottle with his special clear drink. To our surprise, he gave us all of his precious concoction, completely emptying the metal pot. He motioned drink, then sleep, with a big smile on his face. I didn't know how to tell him we had been biking all day and would have no trouble going to sleep, but I gratefully accepted his gift.

Jon and I did not want to overstay our welcome, so we got up to leave. Without any common language, Baatiglee was a most gracious host to a couple of complete strangers who just happened to set up tents nearby. I was so impressed that this Mongolian gentleman with very little to offer gave so freely and generously of what he had. Kindness and generosity are the Mongolian way of life.

We returned to our tents, and I asked Jon if he was interested in drinking the mystery liquid. He said "No," and I agreed with him. We felt obligated to accept Baatiglee's gift although neither of us were interested in actually drinking it. With a surprising amount of guilt, I poured out the bottle.

That night the sky was clear and lit with countless stars. There was no "light pollution" in those remote areas, so the universe was able to show all its glory. The star gazer app on my phone identified Saturn along with many stars I had never heard of before. The beautiful night sky had many more visible stars than we ever had at home. With the temperature just right, it was an outstanding evening.

SEPTEMBER 5: BIKING DAY 11 – BAATIGLEE'S FIELD TO ALTAN-OVOO – 27.5 MILES (317.6 BIKING MILES TOTAL)

I felt sore in my thighs each morning as I began to pedal. After the first mile or so I could find a nice rhythm and work out the soreness. Ibuprofen came in handy too. Our scenery for the day was rural Mongolia at its finest. The vast grasslands, rolling hills, and distant mountains showed the beauty of nature everywhere. A dozen horses were standing in a small, muddy pond by the road, the only water available for miles.

I was looking forward to Altan-Ovoo because our maps showed restaurants, markets, several ger camps, and a hotel. I was thinking about Wi-Fi and a hot shower. On our arrival we saw ger camps with both gers and cabins. Unfortunately, most were closed. We walked around a few camps and found no one in sight, no visitors, and no management. I didn't know if there was a tourist season in this area but, if there was, we were definitely not in it. The hotel referenced on our map was not only closed but looked like it was abandoned years ago. We searched for a while and felt lucky to find two ger camps that were open. We assessed both and decided on the one that had less insects. Neither of us wanted annoying house flies buzzing around all night.

We rode our bikes through the camp and saw a few cabins that looked like they were newly constructed. Jon and I had just begun to discuss the merits of a cabin over a ger when we saw a woman walking toward us. This woman ran the camp, and she kept a close eye on things because her ger was the first one by the entrance. I never got her name, but she looked to be in her mid-30s, the first Mongolian I had seen with reddish hair, although I thought I saw dark roots. Language was a barrier which required each of us to use our Google translators. She showed us around the camp, which had plenty of gers and cabins available as we were the only guests staying there. We chose the upgrade of a cabin instead of a ger. A few extra dollars for "luxurious living" was always worth it.

The cabin was a comfortable A-frame with particle board walls and a concrete floor covered by vinyl planks resembling wood. There was neither Wi-Fi nor showers, or even running water for that matter, but at least there was a bed. Even if it was just a thin mat on a wood frame, it was still better than camping outside. Besides, we had air mattresses to make things more comfortable. The beds seemed short since both my head and feet hit the frame if I stretched out. Jon is about two inches taller than I am, so that looked like an uncomfortable night in store for him. Our hostess brought a large jug of water which I assumed was for drinking. I appreciated the gesture, but I already had a two-day supply of filtered water in my CamelBaks and stayed with what I felt was the safer option. The restroom facilities were a bit lacking. There was an outhouse with a cement floor over a deep pit, with two rectangular slots through which one could straddle, squat, and do their business. Again, there was no running water, so you needed to bring your own hand sanitizer and toilet paper. I wondered what my wife would have thought about this interesting restroom.

After settling into the cabin and unpacking our gear, we took a well-deserved nap before deciding to explore the town. We quickly discovered there was not much to see. The few businesses along the road were closed, perhaps permanently. It felt like walking through a ghost town as I kept looking for tumbleweeds to start rolling through. We walked by a few closed restaurants until we found the only one open. Noodles and mutton seemed to be the food of choice everywhere.

As we were walking back to our cabin, I wondered why the town was so deserted. It was large enough to be on a map, but I could only see a few people. I could not determine how someone would make a living here. Perhaps the younger people were leaving the rural lifestyle and moving to the urban areas for different or better opportunities. This would explain why Ulaanbaatar, the one main city, was growing so fast. I mean no disrespect, but I suppose I was hoping for more from Alton-Ovoo. Perhaps I was disappointed by the out-of-date online information creating inaccurate expectations. I wondered what it would take to revive the town. Tsetserleg is a large town about 20 miles away. There would be a much greater chance of finding Wi-Fi and hot showers there. It's only a day away...

SEPTEMBER 6: BIKING DAY 12 – ALTAN-OVOO TO TSETSERLEG – 17.3 MILES (334.9 BIKING MILES TOTAL)

The fee to stay at a ger camp generally includes breakfast. After about twenty minutes of negotiation, using hand gestures and translation apps, we finally conveyed to our hostess that we were looking for something to eat. I am sure she was as frustrated as we were, answering in a language the other did not understand. But realizing there were no restaurant options, she agreed to make us "pancakes" according to Google translate.

She took us to her ger, which was very cozy with three beds, a television, and a central cast-iron stove for cooking and heating. The stove had a large wok with hot oil. She went to work rolling out dough and making it into pancakes. A quick dip into the hot oil produced our pancake breakfast, along with hot tea and thin pieces of meat. The pancakes looked easy to make and were very good. Another older woman joined us for breakfast, who I believed was her mother. Suddenly, a small head popped up from under a quilt. She was a young child, maybe about two years old, who also enjoyed a good pancake. Her healthy appetite brought smiles from the two women. This grandmother-mother-child family seemed very close. I enjoyed watching their interactions, seeing the unconditional love that a family has for one another.

We paid about $3 for breakfast and rode out of town for the relatively short trip to Tsetserleg. It was an easy ride, passing several gers along the way and countless cattle. The road was mostly flat with only the occasional small uphill grade at times. The grasslands looked greener than the dry, sandy desert areas we had pedaled through a couple of days earlier. It did not take long until we rode under the entrance arch to the city and saw a large, densely packed area with thousands of homes, gers, and buildings, the tallest of which looked like a nine-story apartment building. With a population of just over 21,000 people, Tsetserleg was the largest city we visited since leaving Ulaanbaatar.

I was looking forward to this more urban setting with a hotel to spend the night. There were several hotels, and we chose the Fairfield Guesthouse primarily because of a billboard we passed that advertised their bakery. With an English name, we also hoped to find someone who spoke English. On arrival we found the guesthouse had soft beds, hot showers, good food, and...wait for it...laundry! We were greeted by Caleb, who was originally from Tennessee. Caleb and his wife had just moved to Tsetserleg, I believe from Ulaanbaatar. I was sure he had stories to tell, but he left for the day shortly after we arrived. I hoped I would have time to talk with him when he returned.

After we found our room (with two very comfortable beds!) and unpacked our bikes, we walked a few blocks to a nearby monastery. The Zayiin Gegeen Monastery was built in the mid-to-late 1600s, although much of it was destroyed during the communist era of the 1930s. It was a bit smaller than the other monasteries we had seen, but more historic with only three ancient buildings remaining. It was no longer an active monastery, so there were no monks. The site was now a museum, full of historic artifacts. We walked through the unattended gate into the courtyard. We were the only people there. The three buildings were arranged in a "U" pattern, with two identical two-story temples on each side and a single long temple between them. The smaller temples had areas where the tan plaster had chipped away exposing the stone bricks underneath. The columns, door, and window frames were red with colorful blue, green, and tan artwork as decorative trim. The long temple between the other two may have been red originally, but over time it had faded to brownish yellow. The second level of the temple had three individual buildings that looked like small houses, each topped with a green pagoda-style roof.

All the buildings were unlocked, allowing us to wander through freely. Like the other monasteries, I enjoyed seeing the artwork and historical artifacts everywhere. Some artwork showed scenes of daily life from centuries ago, while others depicted Buddhas and monks. I was always impressed by the intricate designs and the attention to detail by some unknown artisan from years past. Every piece was worthy of preservation in a museum. Buddha statues of all sizes were seen throughout, each painstakingly painted in fine detail.

The monastery was constructed of wood hundreds of years ago. The plank floors would sometimes creak as I walked along. It was late in the afternoon as we were exploring upstairs in one of the buildings when the lights went out. We took that to mean closing time and made our way downstairs just as we heard the unmistakable click of a lock on the door. The immediate thought of sleeping on the cold floor in an empty, old, monastery with the spooky eyes of multiple Buddhas staring down at us all night did not seem like fun. Fortunately, the second thought quickly followed, which was to call out "Hey, hello, we are still in here!" Luckily, the museum guide was still within earshot. She unlocked the door to let us out. A few minutes later we would have had to spend the night in the temple. That would have made for a good story, but we had comfy beds back at the guesthouse.

After our monastery adventure, Jon went back to the guesthouse, and I roamed around the city. There was another monastery high on a hillside which was more modern and looked intriguing, but I was not sure if I wanted to climb all those steps. It reminded me of climbing the many steps of Chichen Itza with Val when we visited the Mayan ruins in Mexico years ago. That was an effort, but absolutely worth it. Curiosity called, and it would only cost a little more thigh burn.

After passing through the entry gate of the Buyandelgeruulekh Monastery, I endured the long climb up the steep hillside. Occasionally turning around, the view of the city improved the higher I climbed. I was intrigued by the densely packed housing along the dirt roads, surrounded by vast stretches of empty hillsides. I thought it odd that people with nomadic roots would live so close together. Near the top was a tall statue of a Buddha with his right hand raised and left arm lower with the palm facing out. The right hand signifies reassurance and fearlessness, while the left hand represents openness and peace. Climbing onward, I finally reached the temple itself. The structure appeared recently constructed, featuring a stone block base, golden doors, and red entry arch highlighted with gold trim. The second level had a small gold building with a golden pagoda roof. Eager to see inside I tried the doors, but they were locked. I climbed all this way and could not get in. I was a little disappointed, but I saw a beautiful temple and the panoramic view from the top was worth every step.

That evening, I heard the gentle sound of raindrops, the first significant rain we had encountered. It was light rain for a few hours, just enough to get things wet but not enough to be a problem. September was supposed to be a dry month, averaging ¼ inch of rain for the month. It was probably a month worth of rain in one day.

I had time in the evening to look for a market to stock up on food. I walked by an elementary school, or maybe a pre-school, with playground equipment for young kids. The building had a mural of Alvin and the Chipmunks painted on the side. I would love to hear what Alvin, Simon, and Theodore sounded like chattering in Mongolian.

Buddha representing fearlessness and peace

SEPTEMBER 7: BIKING DAY 13 – TSETSERLEG TO CAMPSITE 10 MILES WEST OF ZAANKHUSHUU – 28.3 MILES (363.2 BIKING MILES TOTAL)

It was my birthday! I turned 63! The thought occurred to me that if it was September 7th here, but still September 6th in New Jersey where I was born, was it really my birthday? Maybe it was an opportunity to celebrate it twice! All I knew was this trip had aged me, both literally and figuratively! Safely tucked away in my backpack was a birthday card from my wife. I had looked at it frequently but promised myself not to open it until today. A little bit of love in the form of a card was a tremendous gift. It came at the perfect moment in the middle of a long trip so far away from home. I thought about Val all the time, still questioning whether leaving her alone for two months was fair to her. My answer was no, it was not. But she knows my love for adventure and put that above her own needs. It was an act of love, and I love her for it. The most difficult thing about this trip was being away from Val. I often caught myself counting down the time until I would return home, eagerly awaiting that hug at the airport!

During breakfast I had an opportunity to speak with our host Caleb and enjoyed the interesting conversation. He graduated from the University of Tennessee (Go Vols!) and then joined his parents in Ulaanbaatar, both of whom were professors. He worked as an English teacher in the city before moving to Tsetserleg, where he continued to teach. He said it took eight years to learn Mongolian, living in areas where no one spoke English. I would have liked to speak Mongolian, but I didn't want to give it eight years!

Caleb assured us we would have paved roads all the way to Khorgo, except for the steep roads and high mountain passes outside of town. He explained that these dirt roads serve a purpose, providing better traction on the steep grades during icy winters. That was something I had never thought of before but now seems so obvious. Smooth pavement under ice and snow offers no grip. No one wants traction-less tires spinning out of control at the top of a steep mountain pass. For us bikers, dirt roads are much more challenging, but they do have their advantages.

As we were packing the bikes, we met a man called the "French guy." He was also staying at the Fairfield Guesthouse. He spoke a little English and was curious about our bikes and gear. He asked a lot of questions and seemed harmless enough, although I had a strange feeling that I should not leave my bike unattended. Maybe it's my New Jersey roots, or perhaps I have trust issues, but I thought I should keep a close eye on him. As far as I could tell, from translating French, broken English, and a little of my high school Spanish, he had biked all over the world. I didn't know where he had come from, where he was going, or what he was doing. It seemed like he was living alone at the guesthouse. Maybe he was just lonely.

Caleb was right about the roads. The first several miles of dirt road out of Tsetserleg were very steep over the mountain, challenging enough to have to walk the bikes about two miles to reach the top. Brutal. I wished for new thighs for my birthday, or at least some ibuprofen. We came around a very high hill with a smooth rock face that looked nearly vertical. On this face was a line of goats and a few sheep, casually walking across this vertical rock to a grassy area on the other side. A lot of animals are "sure-footed," and these guys are truly experts. There were hundreds of them, and all successfully crossed seemingly without any effort. I was impressed. I wouldn't attempt that even with rock climbing gear, shoes, ropes, and a harness, while they probably walk on rock like that every day.

Once we passed the summit, the rocky dirt road continued for a few miles. It was bumpy, but at least it was downhill. The paved road connected where it was mostly flat, leading to Zaankhushuu, a small village where we stopped for lunch. Most towns had at least one restaurant open for business. Menus were written in Mongolian and some occasionally had English subtitles. I usually looked at the pictures and pointed to something appealing. Just about everything was a combination of noodles and mutton. Maybe it was redundant, but it was tasty hot food that I didn't have to cook. I was OK with that.

A couple of miles past Zaankhushuu we took a break on the summit of a small hill we had just conquered. Our triumphant moment was interrupted by two SUVs that stopped alongside us. The second one had four young men in their early 20s, all happy and smiling while speaking Mongolian. We smiled back, answering their Mongolian with our English. About this time, we noticed a door on the first SUV opened. Among the passengers emerged an older barefoot man with a slight stagger who approached us speaking Mongolian. I could only recognize one word: "vodka." When we explained that we did not have any vodka, he became agitated. He began to wave his arms and started yelling at us in Mongolian. He then staggered over to the second SUV and got into a heated exchange with the other four men. Jon and I looked at each other and thought it was time to leave. The barefoot man then staggered back towards us, again asking for vodka. The men from the second SUV quickly tried to redirect their friend. They escorted him back to the first SUV, pushed him in, then he and his driver left. As the four men returned to their SUV, we nodded to them, thanking them for their help. They nodded back, in such a way that we all understood each other without needing to say a word. We waved goodbye as they drove off following their drunk friend. I was grateful to the guys in the second SUV for both protecting their friend and protecting us. No harm came to anyone, and hopefully he could sleep it off. As we rode off, I wondered how prevalent alcoholism was in Mongolia.

About two hours later, as we were struggling up yet another hill, a car slowed down beside us. Without stopping or saying a word, a man's hand reached out of the window offering me a can of latte coffee. I guess they thought a caffeine boost was needed! While I am not a coffee drinker, I gratefully accepted his gift. Following him was a second car and, in a similar way, a hand reached out to give me a Mongolian Airlines blanket still in the plastic wrap, just as you would find on a plane.

Since it was going to be a chilly night in a tent, I was happy to have it. Jon was right behind me, and they gave him the same gifts. The people in both cars smiled as they drove off, giving a thumbs up of encouragement. Mongolia is a land of nomads. For centuries, people have traveled the country. It is understood that assisting a traveler or someone in need is a noble deed. At some point, we all need a little help. It is the right thing to do and inspires others to do the same. It does for me!

Finally, we decided it was time to set up camp. We found a nice, flat area on top of a hill that looked like home for the night. We set up tents and finished dinner just as the sun was going down and the air became colder. I was so glad I had a warm sleeping bag and a new blanket! I also received a chocolate bar as a gift from Jon. It was a birthday unlike any other I have had.

SEPTEMBER 8: BIKING DAY 14 – CAMPSITE TO CAMPSITE – 27.3 MILES (390.5 BIKING MILES TOTAL)

This was one of our tougher pedaling days. The first five miles were very steep uphill grades, and we walked the bikes about two miles before finding a place we thought we could handle. After very slow progress, we finally made it to the top. Jon's altimeter said it was 6,800 feet. Some of the surrounding peaks had evergreen trees growing naturally on the rocky hillside. It was good to know Mongolia does have some trees! The backside of the mountain was a treat – a relaxing downhill leading to several miles of mostly flat road. Then the wind kicked up. We came up against the strongest wind so far, right in our faces. This certainly knocked several mph off our usual speed, and even gentle uphill grades that were relatively easy became a struggle.

This was a rural area without towns or even small villages nearby. Of course, there was also no Wi-Fi or phone service available. We were in the center of Mongolia now, heading directly west. We encountered more hills and steeper grades than before and had not yet entered the

Altai Mountains further to our west. Although we were still less than halfway through our trip, I thought we were holding up well. Luck had been with us! Without any serious problems or significant injuries so far, I was hopeful that our luck would continue.

We stopped for snacks at what looked like a small ger camp on the side of the road. There was a small main building that had a restaurant sign but was closed. We saw one building, four gers, and 4-5 people milling around. One of them got on his motorcycle and rode off towards a herd of sheep on the hillside. Two other men were very curious about our bikes. We were just as curious about them. They were both in their 30s, one wearing a heavy red and black flannel shirt, black pants, and a black wide-brim hat. The other had a dirty white sweatshirt under a camouflage jacket, with well-worn jeans and a baseball cap. Both men had black boots. We had a limited conversation, mostly with hand gestures and nodding. There was an outside area where cheese was drying in a four-foot-tall mesh bag with six "shelves" also made of netting. Finger sized strings of goat cheese were drying in the sun while being protected from insects and other hungry animals. They proudly showed us their cheese and offered us a taste. It was soft with a delicious, sweet dairy flavor. They allowed us a few photos of them before we continued on our way.

Before the trip I felt cautious about approaching strangers, not knowing if they would be accepting of us. However, nearly every day we have experienced Mongolians being friendly and kind to strangers like us. Being helpful to others is rewarded when others are helpful to you. Buddhism teaches about service to others being one of the first steps on the path to enlightenment. Buddhist philosophy teaches that enlightenment, or Nirvana, is a state of perfect wisdom and compassion, free from suffering. I believe that caring for others is a worthy goal that everyone could achieve.

We pedaled on for a few more hours, rarely seeing another person. This was the most remote area of the trip so far, where the road would lead us to the horizon with nothing but open land on each side. There weren't any towns or houses, and I rarely saw a ger. The only movement we observed was a large herd of yak grazing near the road with their young.

We went a few more miles when we came upon a roadside rest stop. It was going to be another night in tents, and this looked like a good spot to spend the night. It resembled a rest stop you would expect along an interstate highway, the first one we had seen of this kind. It looked newly constructed, with a smooth paved parking lot, outhouse, picnic shelter, and a square fenced-in area for a growing pile of garbage. Trash cans were not very plentiful out in the countryside. Garbage was simply thrown by the side of the road. I saw trash every day while cycling along. We always packed out our trash to dispose of it later, with respect for the beautiful scenery.

We set up our tents, Jon took a nap, and I was journaling at the picnic table when a car stopped. A man walked over and asked me in English where we were going. I introduced myself to him, and he said his name was Boya. We spoke briefly, and he explained he was driving to Ulaanbaatar. I told him we had started in Ulaanbaatar, and he shook his head. I guess he couldn't believe these two idiots had biked all that way. He then placed a handful of chocolate and instant coffee packets on the table as a gift. I offered him some trail mix, which he accepted, and thanked him for his kindness as we said goodbye. I knew Jon would be happy to have the goodies when he woke up.

In the vast fields around the rest stop, I could see in the distance a man and a boy on a motorcycle rounding up a herd of cattle, riding back and forth beeping their horn to move the cattle. The cattle slowly came our way and crossed the road towards a ger a few miles off the road. After the cattle crossed the road, they rode over to the rest stop to greet us. His son, maybe five years old, was riding with him on the motorcycle. They both appeared to be experienced shepherds, with weathered skin, dirty boots, and well-worn clothes. The son looked like he was having the time of his life, riding a motorcycle with his dad. The dad motioned eating and sleeping, which sounded like an invitation for the night. We certainly appreciated his offer, but we were content to stay in our cozy campground, eat a quick dinner, and get to sleep early. Jon and I agreed that we didn't have another few miles left in us, especially uphill to his ger. I gave my chocolate to the boy, which he eagerly accepted. We thanked him for the dinner invitation but had to decline. We nodded, smiled, and waved as he rode back to his herd.

SEPTEMBER 9: BIKING DAY 15 – CAMPSITE TO BELKHI TO KHORGO – 18.6 BIKING MILES (409.1 BIKING MILES TOTAL) 30.4 RIDE MILES (439.5 TOTAL MILES)

The day began cold and damp, probably around 40°F. Thinking it would warm up as we biked, I began my ride and tried to work out the morning stiffness from camping in the overnight cold. As we came to the crest of a hill, I saw another hill in the distance with a dirt road at the top. Remembering what Caleb told us, I knew it was going to be very steep, and we would likely have to walk it. Caleb was right! We walked uphill about a half a mile or more before enjoying the downhill ride.

The late morning continued to be cold, and I was disappointed that the sun could not warm us up. Then it began to rain just enough to make it more uncomfortable. We put on our raingear, which did not help much with the cold, wet conditions. Adding to our misery was a strong headwind beginning to develop. We were lucky we made it to the town of Belkhi right at the height of the storm. We knew Belkhi was a small town that did not offer much, with only a few shops along the main road and homes scattered behind them. There was little activity in Belkhi with nearly every storefront closed. At the far end of the village one restaurant was open. There were no other customers, but they welcomed us to get out of the miserable weather and serve some hot food for lunch. We were grateful because the only other option was to take a different dirt road another 6 km to Teel, which was a slightly larger town but well out of the way. I was relieved not to waste energy on a side trip up dirt roads in the cold rain.

Our original plan was to bike another ten miles and camp out for the night. In cold, wet weather, that did not sound appealing. As we were discussing our options, two men pulled up in a small flatbed truck. A light bulb went on thinking maybe they could give us a ride! At first, they said no, as they were headed in the opposite direction. I guessed they assumed we wanted a free ride. When we indicated we were willing to pay them, they discussed it and we came to an agreed price. They motioned that they needed to go somewhere else first but would return soon.

Just as we finished lunch the two men pulled up in front of the restaurant. We loaded our bikes and gear onto the back of their truck and headed to Khorgo. Yeetchka, the driver, and Bulga, who spoke some English, had come to our rescue. They were both in their 30s and wore traditional Mongolian riding coats, sash belts, and baseball caps. The Nike swoosh on Yeetchka's hat looked a little out of place. I did not notice the alcohol smell on Yeetchka's breath until I was sitting next to him in the cramped cab of the truck. By that time, it was too late to question our decision since he had already begun driving. It was 47 km (29 miles) of bouncing roads from Belkhi to Khorgo. Yeetchka swerved while driving, but I think he was mostly trying to avoid rocks and potholes in the road. Seatbelts may have helped if there were any. Bulga tried to have a conversation with us, which we appreciated given his limited English. Jon and I were relieved to be warm and dry in a truck and, as the weather improved, things were looking up.

A short distance out of town, Yeetchka and Bulga began chattering in Mongolian, then pulled off the road and stopped. They told us to get out. I began to wonder if we were going to be robbed or murdered. Growing up in New Jersey, and having seen "The Sopranos," I was familiar with the concept of "getting whacked." We didn't know what was going on until Bulga pointed in the distance and said "volcano." There was a long-dormant volcano that was a tourist attraction. He pointed to a distant mountain covered by mist and rain. I took pictures since they had gone to the trouble to show us the volcano, but all I saw was mist and rain.

Yeetchka and Bulga, proud Mongolians and superb tour guides

The journey continued until a short time later, when our new Mongolian friends stopped again. This time it was to see a small canyon carved out by a river. It looked like the Grand Canyon of Mongolia! The view was really quite awe-inspiring, as the steep, rocky sides were dotted with trees that had begun to turn orange and yellow. The blue river far below had white streaks of turbulent flow as it rolled over the rocks. I was grateful they stopped to show us this gorgeous scenery. After a few more pictures, we resumed our drive to Khorgo. We thanked our hosts for the combination ride and tour. They were proud Mongolians and happy to show off some of the beauty of their country.

Arriving in Khorgo, my dreams of a cozy hotel with a soft bed, hot shower, and nice restaurant were quickly dashed. The Khorgo Hotel was the only one in town, with no running water and an outhouse in the back. The room had the same basic plywood bed as we had come to expect, with a one-inch mattress. It was, however, still better than sleeping in a cold, wet tent. The lobby doubled as a small dining area where a few other tourists had stopped for lunch. We sat at a table with an Australian, a Canadian, and an Englishman. Our new friends were part of an organized tour group traveling by motorcoach with planned stops. We shared travel stories, and it seemed everyone had an interesting adventure or two to talk about. They thought it a bit odd that we were riding bikes across the country just "winging it." Maybe they were right.

After we finished lunch, I happened to look in the kitchen. There were two large piles of raw meat placed on pieces of plywood laying on the floor. My first thought was that this is where my lunch came from as a queasy feeling hit my stomach. Then I realized if my lunch was not from this meat, it was probably from the previous batch of raw meat that had been on the floor. To make myself feel better, I rationalized that there weren't many flies, and cooking would hopefully kill the germs. I guess they were not too worried about health inspectors coming by.

After our naps, we noticed the rain had stopped, so we had an opportunity to walk around the town. Maybe it was the cold, gloomy weather, but it felt like a sad town with very few people. There were fences around the houses, and all I could see were roofs and chimney pipes. The muddy dirt roads did not help to brighten the mood. We then met a small group of rambunctious young kids, which quickly lifted our spirits. One of them had a cellphone, and we took pictures of them as they took pictures of us. We also found an ATM to replenish our cash supply. Even in the smallest towns, there is usually an ATM.

Along the main road we stopped at a market. It was small, just one room, but appeared well-stocked with food and basic items that people needed. The young woman behind the counter spoke some English, so we asked about catching a ride to Tosontsengel the next day. We had been warned that the road from Khorgo to Tosontsengel traversed through the Khangai Mountains, with very high elevations and much colder weather. Biking the steep peaks would be brutal, and we agreed we were there for fun, not abuse. This small town seemed like a good place to arrange for another ride. The young woman made a few calls and said she found someone who could take both of us, the bikes, and our bags to Tosontsengel in their vehicle. She indicated that he would charge 350,000 MNT (about $100 USD) for the 125-mile trip and drove a Prius. I reminded her to relay to him how much gear we had, surely too much for a Prius. She made another call and said he would get a van instead. I was optimistic that in the morning it would all work out.

Walking back to the hotel, Jon and I got into a discussion about the woman at the market. She looked to be in her early 20s, and I wondered about her future. We weren't sure what, if any, opportunities were available in Khorgo for people her age. Maybe she would be satisfied to stay here and work in the market. Perhaps there were other career paths here, but it seemed like many young people migrated to larger cities, primarily Ulaanbaatar, for education and job opportunities. I was thinking how the older ways of nomads and shepherds appeared to be giving way to more modern business and technology.

SEPTEMBER 10: BIKING DAY 16 – KHORGO TO TOSONTSENGEL – 0 BIKING MILES (409.1 BIKING MILES TOTAL) 123.6 RIDE MILES (563.1 TOTAL MILES)

We had come to expect breakfast to be included at hotels and ger camps. This particular morning, we were told that the lady of the house was sleeping in so no food would be available until after 10:00. We were scheduled to meet our driver at 10:00, so it looked like we were on our own. I suppose most men in Mongolia do not cook. It appeared that gender roles were clearly defined and traditional, with men hunting and women cooking. My guess is if the men were hungry enough, they would figure out how to work a stove. One of the nice things about being self-sufficient was that we had plenty of food in our bags and were not afraid to cook. We dug into our food stash, and it only took a few minutes to whip up a breakfast of oatmeal and raisins. Yum!

We piled up our bags and bikes in front of the hotel and waited for our ride. 10:00 rolled around and into the parking lot arrived...not a van, but a silver Prius. Was this really our ride? The car was in good shape, probably 5-6 years old, with a driver's seat on the right side instead of the left. The driver got out and with a big smile introduced himself as Monko. He seemed friendly enough, around 40 years old, with black hair and wearing a black shirt, black pants, black shoes, and a blue vest. We expressed concern about everything fitting into such a small car. Monko looked at our bikes and gear, gave us a knowing look, and acted like he had it all under control. All the bags and front bike tires barely fit in the trunk and back seat, with just enough room for me to squeeze in. With a blanket on the roof, the bikes were padded with additional blankets and secured with several straps. After Monko's expert packing job, it all fit in the small car with no room to spare. I thought about Jed Clampett's truck in the Beverly Hillbillies, except we had bikes on the roof instead of Granny in a rocking chair.

Jon and Monko squeezed into the front seat while I had just enough room in the back seat. We left the hotel parking lot and proceeded down the road in the wrong direction. As we tried to explain where we wanted to go, Monko gave that knowing smile again and pulled into a gas station for gas and a quart of oil. We then headed out in the right direction, and I noticed the "check engine" light was on. Now I knew why he bought the oil.

The ride to Tosontsengel started out smoothly enough, with flat roads along a beautiful lake. The clear, blue water reflected rolling mountains from the opposite shore. The fluffy white clouds against the

Jon and Monko packing the Prius

Somehow it all fit

light blue sky were a nice addition to the scene. I thought this area would have been an enjoyable bike ride. Soon we hit small hills, then large hills, then the steep high mountain passes. This was the only way through the mountains, with a brutally steep climb. Our little overloaded car was working hard, climbing the dirt roads where we would have been pushing our bikes. After stopping to add more engine oil, we continued climbing until we made it to the top. Jon's altimeter measured 8,600 feet, nearly 2,000 feet higher than where we began the day. Monko stopped so we could enjoy the view. The wind was cold, but the scenery made it worthwhile. There were mountains all around us, with a single thin thread of a distant road crossing the only somewhat flat area of land. That road, the only road, was where we were headed.

I was pleased the Prius with the oil leak made it over the mountain pass. The rest of the ride was mostly downhill, snug but comfortable. We passed small groups of yaks with their long hair well-suited for the cold winter coming soon. The flat grasslands had turned into steep peaks with boulders. As the scenic countryside passed by, the radio played a Mongolian music station. I could not understand the lyrics, but I liked the instrumentation and melody. It was pleasant, sounding like the Asian music played at a hibachi restaurant.

After a few hours we finally made it to Tosontsengel. This was another good-sized city, with a population of 9,000. Tosontsengel is in the Khangai Mountain Range, about 5,600 feet above sea level, and infamous for its brutal winter weather where temperatures can drop to -30s F or below. I was thankful it was still mid-September and not yet winter.

Tosontsengel

We had picked out a few hotels we found online. We liked having options, since what was listed might not be completely accurate, or even open. Our first option was one of those examples. The beautiful photos of a clean, well-maintained hotel, maybe taken years ago, were very different from the run-down state it was in that day. The "lobby" was an empty room and looked like it may have been a dining room in a past life. The floor was torn up, the walls were cracked and bare, and the ceiling needed repair. There were a few dirty boxes laying around covered in dust. The place was eerily empty with no one there to greet us. Being curious, we went upstairs to look at a room. We found dreary rooms with dirty, stained mattresses on beds that looked like they had not been used in years. The only bathroom was downstairs. No running water and a non-working shower did nothing to enhance the overall impression. As we turned towards the door to leave, a gaunt and weary-looking woman entered the room. She offered us a room for the night. Jon and I looked at each other and politely declined.

We drove on to our second choice, a set of small cabins on the hill overlooking the city. Several cabins were unlocked, so we went inside to look them over. They looked like they were recently built with hardwood floors, comfortable beds, pretty wallpaper, and believe it or not, indoor plumbing! We decided this was the perfect place – if we could find someone who worked there.

In front of the property was a large building that looked like a warehouse. There were a few tractor-trailers in the parking lot. I assume we were spotted by someone at the warehouse, and phone calls were made, because a woman in a fancy new car drove up a few minutes later. Her name was Botmy, and she spoke English fairly well. Botmy said her daughter taught her English which I assumed she had learned in school. We arranged to rent a cabin and moved in. The hot shower was only a warm shower at first, which was fine until Jon figured out how to adjust the temperature on the water heater. After that, it felt like home.

Tosontsengel was large enough to meet our needs for markets and restaurants. Even without biking that day, I was just as hungry as if I had. We went to a nearby restaurant and had a very satisfying meat and kimchi dinner. I rarely have an opportunity to eat kimchi, even though it is a healthy food that I like. I thought Korean food might be different here, since we were so much closer to Korea. I was pleased that "authentic" kimchi tasted the same as what we had at home.

After dinner, as the sun was setting behind the mountains, we took a walk to a hilltop to view the town. The blue sky gave way to orange and purple, and the shadows from the buildings began to grow. We walked down to the town on wide dirt roads, mostly seeing solid fences on both sides surrounding small houses. There were plenty of gers in backyards, but most seemed to be unused. It looked like the city dwellers preferred to live in houses. Surprisingly, we saw very few people and, if not for the chimney smoke, the town looked deserted. As it was getting colder and without much to see, we headed back to our cozy little cabin.

The weather was predicted to be bitterly cold the next few days, so Jon and I had a lengthy discussion about our plans. The original idea was to bike west along a northern route toward Ulaangom, the largest city in western Mongolia. From there, we would turn south to finish in Ulgii. We were currently in the Khangai Mountains and would cross several high peaks along this route. The best part about this plan was that it was the shortest route. The problem was that the weather in the mountains had unexpectedly taken a turn for the worse, which was a serious concern. Severe weather can be unpredictable in the mountains. The Siberian High is a brutal blast of cold, dry air that originates in northern Siberia and travels through the mountains of southern Russia and northern Mongolia. It begins in late August and intensifies as the winter months approach. This accounts for the extremely frigid winter temperatures in parts of western Mongolia. Cold, wet weather was expected along our planned route for the next few days. Even though we were traveling well before winter, this was still a rural route with a risk of being stranded by bad weather. There would be several days of long-distance biking without towns or people along the way for shelter or supplies if we encountered any problems. The frigid high-altitude temperatures would make camping untenable, with few options to stay warm. An unlikely, but potentially serious, issue would be food, water, or equipment problems. We were completely on our own, as communications were largely unavailable in these mountains.

Jon and I discussed making a change to our route. The thought of frigid weather in such an isolated region, along with the difficulty of biking through the mountains, was intimidating. There was an option to turn south through a more populated region. This would be a greater distance, eventually requiring us to cross the Gobi Desert before entering the even higher Altai Mountains, but it should be better weather. This seemed like a viable plan, although it would be a completely different route than we had plotted with our satellite imagery maps. We had come to rely heavily on these maps for information about terrain, distance, markets, hotels, ger camps, restaurants and a host of other things. On a different route, these maps would be useless. Our hostess Botmy said she knew a driver who might help us through the local high mountain passes. It was just an option. We would know more in the morning.

Later that night, Jon came into my room saying he felt tight in his chest and was itchy. He did not have any rash or swelling, but his symptoms made me think he was having an early allergic reaction. In my first aid bag I had antihistamine pills and albuterol, which is an inhaled bronchodilator. Allergic reactions involve the release of histamine, which causes itching and tightening of the airways. Antihistamines block the action of histamine, and albuterol helps to dilate, or open, the airways for improved breathing. I gave Jon both, and after taking the pills and a few puffs on the inhaler, he began to improve. I watched him over the next hour or two and was relieved to see he was improving. I wondered what we would do if the first aid bag was not enough, and we had a real emergency. We can't just call 911 for an ambulance. Playing out various emergency scenarios in my head, I tried to anticipate what I would do if things got worse. Tosontsengel had a small hospital, which was reassuring. But if that happened in a remote area, everything would depend on my small medical bag, which was only packed for common things we might encounter. I was not equipped to handle a significant emergency with such limited supplies. This naturally caused a great deal of anxiety, and I worried that I might be unable to help him. Helplessness was a very scary feeling. Fortunately, things quickly improved. I believe reversing it early was important. It is always easier to fix little problems than big problems. This also reinforced our decision to avoid the extremely rural route!

SEPTEMBER 11: BIKING DAY 17 – TOSONTSENGEL – 0 BIKING MILES (409.1 BIKING MILES TOTAL) 0 RIDE MILES (563.1 TOTAL MILES)

Our small cabin had one main room with a sleeper sofa and one bedroom that Jon had insisted I take. I was glad to have it. The bed was the most comfortable one I had slept on since leaving home. We also had a bathroom with a hot shower and a real toilet. Indoor plumbing was a joy, especially after having to straddle a hole in the floor for a toilet. There were several similar cabins that all looked empty, and I believed we were the only people staying there that night. I was happy to be sleeping inside since it hit freezing temperatures overnight. It was cold enough that, in the morning, we had no water due to frozen pipes. This was only a temporary problem, as it warmed up quickly and became a pleasant day to be outside with sunshine, partly cloudy skies, and temperatures above freezing.

Today was planned as a day of rest and to enjoy the restaurants, hot showers, and, most importantly, warm beds with another night of cold weather expected. It also gave Jon and I an opportunity to pour over our maps to continue discussing our options. If we kept the original plan to stay north and head to Ulaangom, we would encounter very cold weather and a 4-5 day stretch of remote camping with no towns or settlements visible on our satellite imagery maps. Turning south would also involve camping, but we would reach Altai City in 3-4 days with a couple of smaller towns along the way. I was always hopeful for a good restaurant and perhaps even an average hotel. Altai City was large enough to have several hotel options. All things considered, turning south seemed like the best option. Bad weather in the mountains could be life-threatening. Turning south would help us avoid the worst of the weather. Although it was a longer distance, the physical task of biking would be tolerable. Aside from pedaling up the steep grades, we thought it might otherwise be enjoyable.

With that settled, I turned my attention to the fragile kickstand on my bike. It was bent out of shape again, and I did not have the tools to repair it properly. I was curious about the big warehouse and tractor trailers located next to our cabins. I thought they might have tools I could borrow. The door to the warehouse was open, so I went in. It reminded me of a Costco or Sam's Club, with rows of metal shelves holding pallets of groceries and household goods. This was Botmy's business, so I guess she was the wholesale distributor for the area. I asked the few people I met but had no luck finding tools. Outside I happened to meet one of the truck drivers who spoke English. I explained my situation, and he led me to his truck. He pulled a toolbox from under the passenger seat and gave me a hammer. I told him I could bring it right back, and he gave me a trusting smile. I thought to myself, this would not happen in the US. I was able to hammer the bend out of the kickstand bracket enough to make it work. It would not support much weight but should work well enough to hold the bike steady while I secure the backpack on it. I returned the hammer, leaving it on the seat in the truck cab since the driver was not around. I appreciated his help and reflected on the generosity of the Mongolian people as I walked back to the cabin.

We enjoyed the rest of the day in Tosontsengel by riding our bikes to the town center, traveling down a two-lane dirt road lined with shops on both sides. It was a busy street, with the dirt worn smooth from all the traffic of cars, bikes, and people. There was an interesting contrast between old and new. Decades old, shack-like buildings stood between new construction with large glass fronts, housing a bank, coffee house, and other businesses. There were several markets where we stocked up on food for the next few days. I was looking for foods that were compact enough to fit in my bags, easy to prepare, and hopefully tasty. I found several items suitable for rural camping over the next few days. Fruits were not plentiful, but dried apricots were a lucky find.

School was letting out, and several kids waved to the strangers on bikes. They seemed to enjoy saying "hello" to the Americans and giggled when we answered back. English is taught in the schools, and several kids could carry on a conversation. It was mostly polite talk, usually asking about where we were from. Since there were not many visitors to this area, people seemed curious and happy to meet us.

Located on the edge of town was an ancient Buddhist monastery referred to as "Old Pagoda," comprised of a large courtyard with several buildings and statues, surrounded by a wall with an elaborately painted open gate. Just inside the gate were rows of prayer wheels - vertical metal columns with writings and symbols, perhaps made of brass or copper. They rotate by turning handles at the bottom. I had seen people praying while turning the wheels. I knew of these prayer wheels and equipped myself with a prayer mantra before starting our trip - "Om Mani Padme Hum" - which roughly translates to "The Jewel in the Lotus." "Om" is the sacred syllable, the primordial sound of all creation, holding within it all that is, was, and ever shall be. "Mani" means jewel, representing altruism, ethical behavior, and patience with others. "Padme" is the lotus, symbolizing wisdom and tolerance. "Hum" refers to the spirit of enlightenment. The prayer wheels appeared to be quite old, and I am sure they have been turned countless times. As I turned the wheel and whispered my prayer, I thought about the unknown number of people over the unknown number of years who have turned it before me. It gave me a feeling of reverence.

We saw several large statues in the courtyard, including one of an elephant, monkey, rabbit, and bird like the one where we had camped several days earlier. This recurring theme holds deep symbolic importance for Buddhists. It was also interesting to see a large statue of a female Buddha. Mongolia seems like a male dominant society, so to recognize a female Buddha with a beautiful statue was refreshing. As I understand it, Buddhas are those who are spiritually awakened and have reached enlightenment, so they can be either male or female. It is unknown how many Buddhas there are. The color, posture, hand and finger positions, objects held, and face of each Buddha represents its identity and attributes. Tara is the most widely known female in Tibetan Buddhism. She is known as the "Leader of the caravans...who showeth the way to those who have lost it."

Inside one of the old temple buildings was a central altar at the back of the room, complete with numerous Buddha statues and candles. On each side were two rows of benches with tables facing the center. They were empty but arranged exactly like the previous monastery we visited, when we saw the monks chanting. A monk was seated at the far left, talking quietly to a man and a woman. I could not tell what they were doing, perhaps a blessing or counseling, but it seemed important. Although this monastery was smaller than the other ones we had visited, it took hours to walk around and see everything.

After leaving the monastery, we started thinking about food. We went to our favorite (and closest) restaurant for dinner. Google translate was helpful but sometimes could not figure out the Mongolian language. Interpreting menus was one such challenge. I focused my phone on the written text of the menu, but some words were lost in translation. Menu items like "guess" (goulash) and "crunchy" (chicken tenders) we eventually figured out. Other items described as "ranch floor," "come on," "be careful," and "sperm" we avoided.

That night I packed up and filtered enough water to last a few days. Botmy arranged for a driver to arrive at 10:00 the next morning and take us over the high mountain pass. This would save us time and, more importantly, lessen the wear and tear on both our bikes and ourselves. It would be no fun walking a bike with 60 lbs or more of gear and water up a steep hill for miles at a time...again. We reminded ourselves we were there to have fun, not abuse ourselves.

SEPTEMBER 12: BIKING DAY 18 – TOSONTSENGEL TO CAMPSITE SOUTH OF TSAGAANCHULUUT – 8.8 BIKING MILES (417.9 BIKING MILES TOTAL) 193 RIDE MILES (764.9 TOTAL MILES)

Our driver arrived promptly at 10:00 and introduced himself as Ardtna. He was a pleasant man in his late 40s in age with short hair, a stocky build, and a bit of a pudge for a belly. Ardtna, of course, had a car - a white Mazda just a little larger than the Prius from two days earlier, also with the steering wheel on the right side. When we showed him our two bikes, Ardtna looked puzzled. Botmy was supposed to tell him about the bikes and gear, but perhaps there was a miscommunication. Ardtna took a moment to think, and in a few minutes the blankets were on the roof of the car along with our bikes. With the bags in the trunk and in the back seat next to me, we were off again to the next town, Uliastai.

The paved road provided a smooth ride for the car, and we enjoyed the scenery. It was still mostly flat with mountains in the distance, and I thought this might have been a beautiful bike ride. Well off the road an occasional ger was seen. Often nearby were herds of cattle or yak. The gentle hills soon became larger, climbing over 2,500 feet in elevation in the first 12-15 miles. I was very happy to be in the car for this part, enjoying the view without burning my thighs. We drove through Uliastai without stopping. It looked like a pleasant little town where it might have been fun to spend a day. The traffic circle at the main intersection had four cows standing in the middle, oblivious to the cars whizzing around them.

Just after leaving Uliastai the pavement ended. Maps showed a major road between Uliastai and Altai City, but did not, however, specify if it was paved. Mongolia continues to pave more roads each year but there are many main roads that remain dirt. We were lucky to get this far on our trip with paved roads nearly the entire way. As we climbed the hills, the roads (and I use this term loosely) became more rutted and rockier. Our satellite images frequently showed dirt roads with adjacent smaller roads, like strands of spaghetti all going in a similar direction. Having been on these roads, I now understand why. If a section of road becomes too difficult, just drive around it and make a new path. A driver has options to choose the least bad road.

Our little Mazda climbed a long way. I believe it would have taken a week or more to walk our bikes up those mountain passes. Eventually we came to the summit at an elevation of 8,400 feet. From the mountain top, there was a picturesque moment overlooking a valley with one winding road that seemed to go on forever. I was hoping the downhill would be smoother but, no, it was just as rocky and bumpy. I was also looking forward to pavement, but the rutted dirt road just continued. Without seatbelts, we were all literally bouncing off the seats. I worried about how the car was holding up. It was a well-built car, but it took a lot of punishment.

The scenery was beautiful, becoming more mountains with less plateaus. It was dry with sandy soil and felt like a desert. Although the land was steep and rocky with scrub vegetation, we still encountered herds of sheep and goats, which tended to herd together. At one point we had to stop for horses to move off the road, and then another time for yaks. I don't know much about yaks, but they quickly became my favorite animal. They looked like hairy cows with an attitude. A yak will stare you down in the middle of the road, expecting you to go around them. They don't care if you beep the horn or rev the engine. They move when they feel like it.

There was a small Buddhist monument near one of the peaks where we took a break. Three beautiful Buddas were carved into the rock face, along with prayer wheels and a small shelter with a table and bench. Next to the shelter was an area for prayer flags, and it looked like hundreds were left there by travelers wishing for a safe journey. It looked like a popular place to stop on this remote, rocky road. We were only there for fifteen minutes or so, and a couple of cars stopped during our short visit.

Yaks - hairy cows with attitude

We came to Tsagaanhayrhan, our agreed stopping point but, with the terrible road conditions, we convinced Ardtna to drive us farther for a little cash bonus. The next "town" was Tsagaanchuluut, which was almost 50 miles away. This would not only save time, but also spare us a lot of abuse from the constant pounding of washboard dirt roads.

When we arrived at Tsagaanchuluut, which was a tiny village off the main road, we were basically in a desert. It reminded me of the south-western US with sagebrush bushes, little grass, and mountains surrounding it all. We asked if we could pay Ardtna to take us further down the road but after five hours driving there, and another five hours to drive back to Tosontsengel, I think he had enough. He would drive that same rocky washboard dirt road back home again. I'm sure he drives these kinds of roads frequently and I don't understand how his car stays together. A car repair shop would be a great business opportunity there.

After Ardtna helped us unload the car he took our pictures, likely for proof that two idiots paid him to drop us literally in the middle of nowhere. He then wished us well as he waved and drove off. I had a bit of a "oh no what have we done" feeling about being stranded in a desert, but there was only one dirt road, and we knew Taishir and Altai were at the end of it.

We reassembled our bikes and were in the process of packing our gear when a small truck pulled up. A man emerged speaking rapidly in Mongolian, who appeared curious and happy to see us. His wife and small child remained in the truck. He helped me steady my bike in the soft dirt while I strapped the backpack and equipment bag onto the cargo rack. He carefully looked over my work making sure everything was tight. Jon offered trail mix to him along with his wife and child. We thought he might offer us a ride, only to say no when Jon motioned about putting a bag in his truck. He indicated he was going the other direction. Since we were ready to start biking again, we thanked him and parted ways. I thought another ride would be great but, in a strange way, I didn't mind pedaling again. We were here to bike across Mongolia, and even though rides were a necessity to get through some of the extremely demanding terrain, in some ways it felt like cheating. I enjoyed biking, and pedaling in this land was so unlike anything I had experienced before.

The dirt road was flat but slow because of the soft, sandy soil. The dry yellow grass stretched out for miles. Four camels were watching us from about 200 yards away. They were close enough to see us but far enough away to feel safe. I don't think they were interested in us anyway, and would probably have walked away if we approached.

We biked for a few miles until around 6 p.m. and found a place to set up our tents for the night. In the desert it gets cold quickly after sunset, so having tents set up, sleeping bags ready, and dinner completed before nightfall was important. We were on our own for the next few days, so a warm sleeping bag sounded inviting. Before I went to sleep, I peeked out of the tent to see a beautiful star-filled night sky. My star identification app was busy naming everything in sight, including a planet or two. Without city lights obscuring the sky, I could see the Milky Way spreading out into infinity. It was awe-inspiring and humbling at the same time.

Sometime in the middle of the night, I was awakened by a loud snorting noise just outside the tent. I laid there in my sleeping bag and wondered what kind of creature would make that noise. I debated whether I should go outside to look, or maybe just poke my head out of the tent, but decided I was too tired to get out of my warm sleeping bag. The next morning, I asked Jon if he heard the noise. He did, and he thought it was a camel. It probably was, but neither of us felt like getting up to look.

SEPTEMBER 13: BIKING DAY 19 – CAMPSITE TO TAISHIR – 26.5 BIKING MILES (444.4 BIKING MILES TOTAL) 0 RIDE MILES (791.4 TOTAL MILES)

The day began in a beautiful way with sunshine and cool temperatures - not cold, but just right. I made my usual camping breakfast of hot tea, oatmeal with raisins, dried apricots, and my last orange purchased in Ulaanbaatar. I was surprised it had lasted so long and was still juicy.

We biked through the most remote areas we had seen so far. There was no internet, Wi-Fi, or ability to connect with a cell tower, so I had no contact with Val. It would have been a pleasant way to end my day if it was possible. The last time we spoke, I let her know we would be remote and likely out of contact for a while. Somehow Jon got a text out to let his wife know we made it through another day. He was lucky to get that one text out because there were no other texts, incoming or outgoing, getting through anymore.

For most of the day we saw no one. There were plenty of sheep, maybe some horses, and an occasional ger tucked away in the mountains, but no people or cars. I reflected on my usual days in the office when I was working, busy with something every minute. Now here we were, Jon and I, with all the time in the world. It felt liberating, but at the same time a bit weird because it was not what I was used to. People are social beings, and I wondered how the shepherd in that single ger on top of a mountain coped with the loneliness of each day.

The practical side of me wondered how I would handle a significant injury or problem with a bike. How would we get help? Then my mind eased into my current surroundings, and I allowed myself to enjoy the solitude. The terrain was mostly flat with gentle hills between the higher peaks. The smooth sections of the dirt road were some of the best biking so far. We were just riding through nature without concern for anything. The only sounds came from the bike and the gentle breeze.

There were no road signs but, with only one dirt road, we were pretty sure we would not get lost. Google maps was a helpful tool and worked even when there was no internet. It gave us a rough idea of how far it was to Taishir, our goal for the day. That would put us only one day out of Altai City, where we knew of a luxury hotel with hot showers. The plan was to then enjoy a full day off relaxing. We were glad when we finally saw telephone poles in the distance because that was a sign of civilization. Those poles would lead us directly to Taishir, which was the only village for many miles. The road twisted and turned, but the telephone line usually ran in a straight line which helped us maintain our heading.

All too soon, our blissful day began to turn on us. The smooth dirt road changed to rock and sand, then rutted like a washboard. The enjoyable ride became challenging, and then awful. The constant slow struggle of biking in the sand was almost as bad as the jarring of every unavoidable bump we hit. The pounding took a toll on both the bikes and the riders. Next, the weather turned cold and damp. We knew that rain was coming. Cold and wet was a bad combination.

After completing a particularly rocky stretch of dirt road, Jon blew his rear tire tube. No worries, I thought, since we were prepared with spare tubes. We put our rain gear on and proceeded to take Jon's trailer off so we could get to his tire. In the middle of all this a Jeep pulled up and stopped. It was the same man we met yesterday when Ardtna dropped us off. This was our second encounter with this kind man, and I regretted that neither Jon nor I could remember his name. Still smiling and seeming glad to see us again, he came out of the Jeep (a different vehicle from yesterday) and was eager to help Jon change the tube. I tossed Jon a tube given to us by Bimba at the bike store in Ulaanbaatar where we purchased the bikes. Unfortunately, it was the wrong tube. It was the correct 29 inches, but it had the larger Schrader valve which would not fit through the hole in the wheel rim designed for the smaller Presta valve. This was concerning as I expected more tubes might blow, and my three extra tubes were all useless. Jon dug through his bags and found only one tube with the correct valve, so the crisis was averted for now, but we had no extra tubes for the next blowout. Most of these towns do not have a bike store, or anywhere else for that matter, to buy extra tubes. All we could do was hope we didn't blow another tube. With our repairs completed, our friend returned to his family in the Jeep, and we returned to our bikes.

Soon after we began pedaling on our rocky road, the rain began. Thinking we would be in the dry season when I packed, I had underestimated my need for rain gear. My thin, lightweight poncho folded tightly and was ideal for packing. Unfortunately, it did not provide as much weather protection as I had hoped, especially while trying to ride the bike. I was envious of Jon's rain jacket, which was much better than my leaky poncho. We still had many miles to go, being cold, wet, and biking on terrible roads. All we could do was to push on. The goal was Taishir and we were going to make our goal. Anything less was not an option! Eventually we came to the crest of a hill. In the distance I saw a small area with buildings, which could only be Taishir. It was still a few miles farther, but now it was in sight!

We made it into Taishir cold and wet but thrilled to be finished for the day. We rode down the main street past closed businesses, looking for a hotel and restaurant. The only business open was a small market about the size of a bedroom. There were no customers, and the only person in the building was the man behind the counter. With our hands we motioned eating and sleeping to the clerk. He motioned back that there was no restaurant and pointed in a direction where we could find a hotel.

We explored the area but had no luck finding a hotel. We flagged down a young man on a motorcycle and motioned "sleep" to him. He also pointed in the same direction. We continued up and down the street with no obvious hotel in sight. We saw a teenager who was watching us, obviously seeing two lost tourists who needed help. The boy must have been about 16 and appeared eager to assist. We again motioned "sleep" to which he nodded "yes" and took us to a nondescript building. The long, gray one-story building with a green metal roof had one orange door for an entrance but no signage to let anyone know what it was. There was a small fence along the pavestone sidewalk separating it from the overgrown, weed-filled yard. I went inside, past large bags of sand in the foyer, into the dark, empty building. Motion-sensor lights lit up a long hallway with an orange floor. A red carpet runner with gold designs was in the middle of the hallway. Closed doors along the hall could have been rooms with beds, but the only open door was at the end of the hallway where the lights did not work. The hotel was eerily quiet, as if we were the only ones there. In the dim light I looked upon a spartan room with minimal furnishings. An older woman soon appeared, who looked to be in charge of the place. She did not speak English, so we motioned "sleep" to her. She motioned for us to follow, leading us to a room down the hall and knocked on the door. A younger woman answered who knew a few English words. She quickly understood we wanted a room for the night. We were shown to a room with two one-inch mattress beds, one table, and two chairs, which was an upgrade from the room we had just seen. The red linoleum floor was spotlessly clean. A mural of two houses along a lake with mountains in the background was painted on the wall where the wallpaper had peeled away. This "hotel" could use a few renovations but was just what we needed.

When we asked about food, the young woman nodded "yes." A pitcher of hot water soon arrived. I was concerned our request for food was lost in translation. I enjoyed a cup of tea, but we were still in search of real food in a town without restaurants. Since we had food with us it really wasn't that big of a problem, but restaurant food is (usually) better than camping food. I also had an issue having lost my reading glasses somewhere in all the flat tire commotion. I had them in my shirt pocket and I guess they fell out while I was bending over. They were not expensive, but I liked how they looked. I had a small magnifying glass and reader sunglasses, which would have to do. There were no Walmarts in Mongolia to get new ones.

A short time later, a sweet grandmotherly woman knocked on our door. She was probably in her late 60s, a little over 5 feet tall, wearing a floral shirt and carrying a tray with a large bowl of hot noodles with meat and vegetables. We were surprised and grateful as she dished it out for us. Jon offered to help her, but she took one look at his grubby camping spoon and gave a look of mild disgust that was priceless. Jon quickly cleaned his spoon, and then she accepted it. I thought it was ironic that in this old, run-down hotel, the spoon had to be clean to touch her food. But it was right to give respect for her food, as it was delicious. She was not about to let that nasty spoon touch her fine cooking. It was a wonderful meal prepared by a wonderful woman.

After dinner we took a short walk around town. I noticed our hotel did not have running water or a bathroom. Luckily (I guess) for us there were several outhouses with the missing middle floorboard scattered around town. They were simple, small wooden structures built over a large hole in the ground. I am not as agile as I once was because sometimes when I squatted, I would need to balance myself with one hand on the floor. Believe me when I say, the wooden floor was not the most sanitary place to be touching. Some people had difficulty properly hitting that hole in the floor. I tried not to think about what germs would grow in a laboratory Petri dish from a culture of the floor. I always had to bring my own toilet paper and hand sanitizer. I was also incredibly paranoid about dropping my cellphone down the hole. My phone was a vital lifeline in many ways. Maybe I could just wait until we get to a real bathroom in Altai City tomorrow!

We walked down the main street past an ornate Buddhist monument capped by a cupola, complete with prayer wheels and two prayer benches for kneeling. The small fence around it was covered in prayer flags. It did not take long before we were noticed by the local kids. They were eager to say "hello" which may be the only English word they knew. They were just like us, with "san banoo" (hello) being one of the few Mongolian words we knew. One boy around eight years old was quick to show off his bow (without arrows) and pose for a few pictures. The others soon followed, wanting us to take pictures.

Three future Mongolian warriors

We stopped by the only open market and bought a couple of beers. When we returned to the hotel, we saw two men putting in new light bulbs at our end of the hallway. I suppose someone called the "maintenance department" for us.

This hotel may have had some faults, but it did have Wi-Fi. The best part of the day was getting a call through on WhatsApp to Val and the kids. Since I was almost ready for bed, I knew Val would be waking up at home. It was always comforting to know that she and Ziggy (our dog) were doing well.

SEPTEMBER 14: BIKING DAY 20 – TAISHIR TO ALTAI CITY – 32.1 BIKING MILES (476.5 BIKING MILES TOTAL) 0 RIDE MILES (823.5 TOTAL MILES)

Brutal day biking. It was uphill most of the day on washboard dirt roads of sand, loose gravel, and rocks, with just enough headwind to make it annoying. It was an 8-hour day biking along at a blistering pace of 4 mph.

On the brighter side, it was another day in the rural countryside with lots of open space and surrounding mountains. To our west they were snowcapped, which looked pretty but also reinforced our decision to turn south and avoid the colder weather. We did not see or speak to another person all day. Maybe six cars passed us on the "road," giving double takes from people who likely do not see bicycles out this far. We saw what looked like a mining operation in the hills, but it was too far away to see what they were doing. We remembered the map showed a copper mine somewhere in that area, so that might have been what we saw.

At the top of a long hill stood a Buddhist monument with a small ovoo. It looked similar to the others where travelers could stop and pray for a safe journey. The numerous prayer scarves tied around the ovoo were frayed from the constant wind. Nearby in a large circular monument there was a portrait of a woman in formal traditional dress and head piece. The image showed her standing in front of the Taishir hydroelectric dam, which provided power to the region. The words in the monument were in traditional Mongolian script written vertically, which predates the Cyrillic alphabet by centuries. Mongolian script was used even before the days of Chinggis Khaan.

The cool temperatures of the morning became colder as the wind picked up. Two menacing dark clouds formed on the horizon, the first moving east fast enough to bypass us, but the one behind it looked like it was coming our way. There were distant rumbles of thunder but no lightning that we could see. A slight drizzle turned into light rain, so it was time to put on the leaky rain poncho again. We had already experienced more than the usual amount of September rainfall, and now we were getting more. As the rain increased, the temperature decreased to the low 40s, heading towards freezing later that night. It was made even worse by adding wind and the potential for lightning. Altai City was still about 10 miles away, and it was not a night for camping. We briefly discussed our options of putting up tents to shelter from the storm, or forging ahead and trying to make it to Altai City. We decided on the latter. It was going to be a race against the weather.

As we pedaled on, I began to hear slight clicking noises on my bike helmet and noticed tiny white bits on the ground. It had started to hail, with some hitting me in the face. I had to pull my neck gaiter up over my nose for protection. With my helmet, sunglasses, and neck gaiter, my head was still wet but protected as much as possible. The rain and hail increased for the next mile or two as the second black cloud closed in on us from the west. I was hopeful we could reach Altai City before the worst of the weather hit us, which was no guarantee on these terrible dirt roads.

The miles churned slowly over the rocky roads made worse by the horrible weather. After what seemed like an endless day of miserable biking, we finally reached the crest of a hill where in the distance a city appeared. I felt like I was seeing the "promised land" after our trek across the desert. Altai City was still far off but at least we could now see it. It seemed painfully slow trying to reach our goal. All I could think of was reaching our fancy hotel for a hot shower and a good meal. Altai was a large city, and we understood it was quite modern. It was something we looked forward to.

Wet weather approaching Altai City

The rain slowed a bit as the dark clouds appeared to move behind us. Of course, there were more hills as we approached the city, but these were much smaller than the ones we had tackled throughout the day. We were both cold, wet, tired, and hungry, which drove us to make it through this final push.

Just after entering the city, we were greeted by a modern-looking five-story hotel. Although it was probably built in the days of Soviet Russian control, it still looked like paradise to me. This was the kind of hotel that I knew had a good restaurant and indoor plumbing just by looking at it. Jon went inside to book a room while I stayed outside propping up my top-heavy bike with the broken kickstand against the building and out of the rain. As I walked into the hotel, Jon was standing in the middle of the lobby, dripping all over the clean marble floor. He told me they had no rooms available. At first, I thought he was joking, but in fact they were fully booked. As we both stood there dripping on their beautiful, shiny floor, the woman at the front desk pointed down the road to another hotel which looked about a mile away. Since we were both hungry, and the restaurant was just off the lobby, we sloshed our way over to get some food. I ordered two entrees of the usual noodles and meat and was hungry enough to eat them both.

I did not think I had another mile in me, but a good meal and thoughts of a hot shower made it happen. We arrived at the next hotel only to be told they were also fully booked. We were told a mining convention had come to town and booked all the available hotel rooms. The woman at the reception desk made a call and found a room available at yet another hotel which fortunately was nearby. We biked over and, sure enough, we found our room for the night.

The Altai Hotel was an old building, three-stories high, painted green and white. We were happy to finally have a room but also understood why, during a huge mining convention, this hotel still had rooms available. It was not the kind of place with white marble floors.

We slogged our rain-soaked gear upstairs and unpacked it to dry. We asked if they had a laundry service which caused a bit of a commotion among the three women who worked there. After much discussion in Mongolian, one of them said they would do our laundry for 20,000 MNT, or about $3 USD each. That seemed like a fair price, so we agreed. All I had to do now was find that hot shower I was looking forward to. Jon went first and with an annoyed look announced there was no hot water. I tried to adjust the faucets but was also disappointed. Jon brought the dirty laundry bags downstairs and mentioned there was no hot water. The woman went to a back room and flipped a switch, saying we should have hot water soon. Maybe she flipped the wrong switch, but we never had any hot water. So much for that shower idea. At least we were going to have clean clothes. Later that evening our clean laundry was delivered, sitting in a laundry basket still wet. Clothes dryers are uncommon since the arid climate dries everything and electricity is expensive. The hotel room was large enough to spread out all our wet clothes, and we hoped by morning they would be dry. Dispirited but too tired to care, it was time for bed!

SEPTEMBER 15: BIKING DAY 21 – ALTAI CITY – 0 BIKING MILES (476.5 BIKING MILES TOTAL) 0 RIDE MILES (823.5 TOTAL MILES)

A day off! Feeling entitled to a little break, we decided to enjoy all that Altai City had to offer. Near our hotel there was a bakery/coffee house that seemed to cater to English-speaking people. Their signage and menus were in English, and their walls had pictures of New York City on them. It made me wonder, other than Jon and me, how many locals had been to New York City. I had pizza, chicken tenders, and a drink for brunch.

There was a small window in the back wall from which a cake or two would suddenly appear. These cakes were masterpieces - beautifully decorated and looking delicious. The next time the window opened, I had a chance to peek inside. There were half a dozen women busy with mixing bowls and ovens. There was a large table where the magic happened, with a few cakes in different stages of frosting and decoration. I didn't think cake would go well with my pizza, but I was tempted. I would have to come back later.

Returning to our hotel, I saw a horse in the street also walking to our hotel. He decided the grass in front of our hotel looked like a tasty treat. I watched him eat for a few minutes until a woman from the hotel came outside yelling at the horse. He tried to ignore her, but she was persistent and eventually shooed him away.

Our chore list for the day was short. All we really needed to do was find a way to reach our next goal, Khovd. Between Altai City and Khovd lies about 250 miles of the Gobi Desert. We were on the northwestern edge of the Gobi, the largest desert in Asia. It borders the Altai Mountains to the west, which was the direction we were going. Roughly 1,000 miles long and 600 miles wide, the desert straddles both southern Mongolia and northern China. The word Gobi means "waterless place" in Mongolian. The soil was rockier and coarser than sand. The road was paved, so cycling wouldn't be too bad, but there were no real towns along the way. That meant no communication with home and the need to pack 10-14 days of food and water. Jon and I discussed the situation and decided to look for alternatives.

We had seen big, modern motorcoaches traveling through Altai City, and since Altai and Khovd are both big cities, we knew there must be a way to get there. There was a bus station a few blocks away, which we believed should make things relatively easy. At the bus station window, we asked for two tickets to Khovd. We were told there was no bus to Khovd - they only sold bus tickets to Ulaanbaatar. I knew there was a bus that traveled between Ulaanbaatar and Ulgii, which I thought passed through both Altai City and Khovd, but the woman at the window said "No." She suggested we ask at the market, pointing in a general direction down the street. We wandered that way, wondering what market she was talking about.

On the street there was a woman and young girl walking nearby, perhaps a mother and daughter, and we asked them for directions. "C" was older, and Nomio, the younger one, spoke some English. With the help of Google translate and broken English, they understood what we wanted. They led us to the "market," which was an open-air event in a small plaza where people sold goods out of the back of their trucks. Among the vendors were four pickup trucks with raw meat in the back. We were told it was fresh horse meat for sale as they proudly butchered it in front of us. I nodded and declined.

Inside the building we found the public transportation booth. The woman at the desk also said there were no busses to Khovd and gave me a phone number to call for assistance. We called the number and, with the translation help of Nomio, were told they had a driver who would take us, our bikes, and bags to Khovd for a total of 200,000 MNT, or about $30 each. Considering it's a five-hour drive each way, I thought that was a bargain. Nomio and C asked for our Facebook page information and email to keep us informed of any last-minute changes.

After the driver was arranged to pick us up at 9:00 the next morning, Nomio sent me a message on Facebook saying she knew this driver and he "seems like a bad person to trust a little" meaning that he will ask for more money. Realistically, $60 to drive both of us with all our gear five hours across the Gobi Desert was pretty cheap, so I anticipated the price might change.

With the transportation issue out of the way, Jon and I split up so I could try to replace the reading glasses I had lost in the flat tire fiasco. Since I could find cheap readers in any pharmacy or Walmart store at home, I thought these would be easy to replace. After checking several places and coming up empty, I was told to go to the local hospital. I struggled to find the hospital, wishing for a big blue "H" hospital sign to guide me.

I finally discovered a nondescript, two-story building that Google maps designated as the hospital. I saw no signage that would suggest any type of business, much less a hospital. I checked doors along the front of the building, but they were all locked. Walking around the side of the building, I found an unlocked door with a small sign above it that read "Hospital" in English and Mongolian. I entered what looked like a deserted reception area. I tried to translate the directory sign, but Google was offline. I stepped outside to check my Wi-Fi connection and heard the cleaning woman lock the door behind me. I knocked, but she wouldn't open it. I continued around to the back of the building and located another unlocked door. I entered and wandered into the emergency department. A nurse there agreed to help and walked me to the ophthalmology department. She said the hospital was closed for lunch and gave me a phone number to call. A woman with broken English answered, saying they would reopen at 3:00, which was three hours away. I found a small waiting area just outside the ophthalmology department. With nowhere else to go, I waited.

As time went by a few people gathered, and then some more. By 3:00 a crowd of 20 or more people were waiting with no sign of a healthcare provider. Finally, a woman in a white coat approached carrying a key ring and opened the door. Through my translator app I told her what I wanted. She knowingly nodded and must have been the woman I spoke to on the phone. With a waiting room full of patients, she led me away down the hallway, down the stairs, across the lobby, out of the hospital, across the courtyard, into a second building, down the hall, out the back of the second building, crossed the street, and continued to yet another building with a sign shaped like an eye but with a "closed" sign on the door. She unlocked the door and went behind a counter, pulling out two pairs of reading glasses. I picked one, paid her 20,000 MNT ($6 USD), and it was done. I was amazed that the doctor would take the time to help me purchase glasses with an office full of patients. I thanked her and we parted ways. She went back to her busy afternoon, and I left with my new glasses.

As I walked away, I thought about my career as a busy pediatrician seeing 30-some patients each day. I believe most health care providers would like to spend more than 10-15 minutes with each patient, but time does not always allow for that. I always enjoyed having a little extra time with the kids whenever the opportunity presented itself. Unfortunately, the US system is not set up that way. I wondered how much I had delayed the doctor's schedule with my quest for reading glasses. I felt guilty having caused a delay for every patient she saw that afternoon.

After getting back to the hotel, I remembered my bike didn't feel right coming into Altai yesterday. It seemed to be off-balance with a wobble. I had the time to check it and found one of the main bolts for the support bracket of the cargo rack had sheared off. All the pounding of washboard roads and 70 lbs of weight was just too much for that poor little bolt. There was no way the cargo rack would now hold without the support bracket. Without the proper tools to fix it, I had to improvise. I had duct tape and cable ties in my tool bag because they can repair almost anything. It wasn't pretty, but I found a way to secure the support bracket to the bike frame. I was quite pleased with myself, first for packing things that I thought I would not need but packed anyway, and second for figuring out a way to use those things to fix a significant problem. It made me think of the movie "Apollo 13" where NASA engineers had to bring home a crippled spacecraft with whatever duct tape and cable ties they happened to have in the space capsule. The remainder of the trip should have paved roads, so hopefully it would survive the abuse of biking for the next several days.

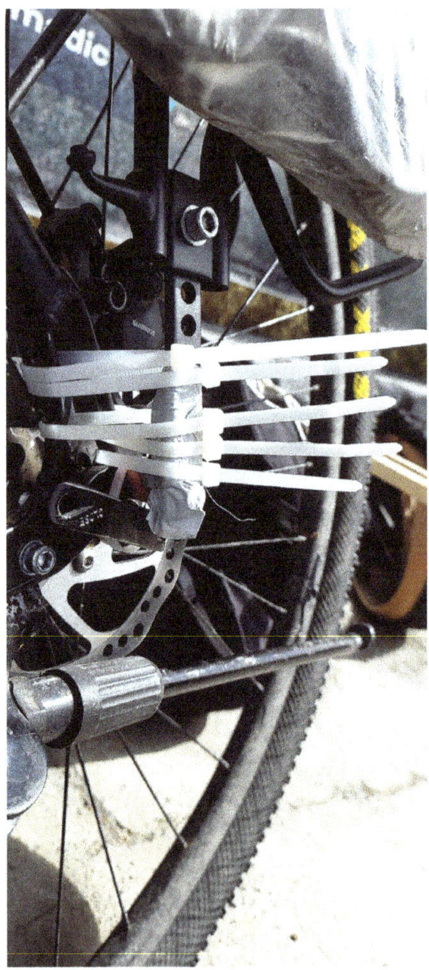

Duct tape and cable ties can fix anything

With a ride to Khovd now arranged, we planned our last biking segment from there to Ulgii. Even though roads were paved, it was still about 145 miles over mountains. There were no significant towns along the way, only a few small settlements that hopefully would have a roadside diner. A hotel would be wonderful, but Google couldn't find one. Jon and I agreed early on that if there was ever a hotel available, that would be our first choice. The weather would also be a key factor with temperatures expected to be no higher than 50°F during the day and freezing at night. We would be entering the Altai Mountains at around 6,000-7,000 feet in elevation. This would put our altitude as high as Mt. Mitchell (6,684 feet) in North Carolina, the highest peak east of the Rocky Mountains. Weather information was crucial. We could check the latest weather predictions when we get to Khovd. The snow-capped mountains ahead of us were getting closer and looked very intimidating.

SEPTEMBER 16: BIKING DAY 22 – ALTAI CITY TO KHOVD – 0 BIKING MILES (476.5 BIKING MILES TOTAL) 275 RIDE MILES (1098.5 TOTAL MILES)

All our drivers so far have been very professional, arriving on time with the necessary blankets and straps needed for our bikes and gear. Today, however, the "untrustworthy" driver failed to show up at the designated time of 9:00. Twenty minutes later I was on Facebook messenger to Nomio asking her to contact him. She said she would try to help, so all we could do was wait.

It took another twenty minutes until our driver finally arrived. He stepped out of his Prius looking bewildered at our bikes and gear bags. When we had communicated our needs to Nomio, we said multiple times that we had two men with two bikes and baggage. I was sure this information had been relayed correctly, as it was on our last Prius adventure. Other drivers were prepared, but today's driver looked clueless. We opened the back of his car and found it full of large speakers and stereo equipment, with no room for our things. With the help of Nomio and a bystander who happened to be able to translate, phone calls were made.

A second car soon pulled up with roof racks, but the driver said he wouldn't take us to Khovd because it was too far. Our ride across the desert looked like it was not going to happen. Jon and I did not want to bike through the desert, and began to discuss what other options, if any, we had. Eventually a third car came with a woman who may have been a supervisor, and talked briefly to the two drivers. The second driver left, and the supervisor left, without telling us any information. The only good sign was that the first "untrustworthy" driver was still there, meaning he was still willing to take us to Khovd.

A short time later a fourth car came, of course a Prius, and we realized we each now had our own car and driver. Our bikes and gear easily fit in both cars, but the price jumped from 200,000 MNT to 500,000 MNT. All things considered, it was still worth $70 each to drive for five hours, especially since it was our only way to get to Khovd. I would much rather pay the drivers than bike for two weeks across the Gobi Desert.

So, we loaded up both cars, paid the drivers, and we were on our way. It was mostly a quiet ride, since the entirety of my Mongolian was "hello" and "thank you." I shared my trail mix with my driver, and he shared his candy with me. There was Mongolian music on the radio, and we amused ourselves trying to get a fly to go out the window. The driver and I both tried to get the fly to the top of the window, then open the window to suck it out. I must give that fly credit since he was faster than we were. As soon as the window moved, he flew down to safety. Our game went on for about an hour before the insect finally disappeared out the window.

We rode through a section of the Gobi which was unlike the pictures of sand dunes I had seen. Those areas were further southeast. This area looked more like the deserts in the southwest US, similar to Arizona or New Mexico, with flat land, scrubby vegetation and snowcapped mountains in the distance. The soil was a dry sand and dirt mixture. We passed a few camels but otherwise there was no sign of any grazing cattle, sheep, or goats previously seen in the lower grasslands. The small amount of scrub vegetation would never support a grazing herd.

The speed limit signs of 80 km/hr (50 mph) seemed to be merely a suggestion. The speedometer in the car hovered in the mid 130-140 km/hr (80-90 mph) range for most of the trip. With no seatbelts in the car, I tried to rationalize that at least the roads were mostly straight. At one point we approached the crest of a hill and were unable to see beyond it. The driver decided this would be a good time to pass the car in front of us. We did pass safely, and maybe somehow the driver knew it was safe, but I think we were more lucky than safe.

Roughly midway through the trip, we stopped at a gas station. It turned out to be the only gas station on this road. There were no other signs of civilization for hundreds of miles. No towns, no gers, and rarely another car. One little station to prevent people from running out of gas in the middle of the desert. I thought it would take most of the day for a gas truck to make the long journey here and back from wherever it came from. And what about the guy who worked there? Does he live here or commute to work every day?

After five long hours of driving, we arrived in the city of Khovd. It was significantly larger than I had anticipated. Khovd had a population of about 30,000, or about twice the size of Altai City. We needed the help of Google maps to find the Steppe Hotel, our goal for the day. The Steppe Hotel was the nicest place we stayed in during our entire trip. We were greeted by clean marble floors, comfortable rooms, and indoor bathrooms that actually had hot running water. Five-star accommodations all the way!

After we unloaded our things, the "untrustworthy" driver asked us for an additional 20,000 MNT. We had already paid more than double the original agreed price and, having been warned he would do things like this, we said no. I still struggle with this decision. It was only a few more dollars for a ride that helped us tremendously, but it felt like he was trying to cheat us after agreeing to terms. If he asked for it up front, we would have paid it. Nomio warned us about him, and I did not want to encourage his bad behavior.

Jon and I spent the afternoon walking around Khovd, which was an interesting city. There were buildings of various sizes and ages. Several construction cranes dotted the skyline. Residents lived in houses, shacks, and gers, all surrounded by walls or fences. We found a street market with a line of vendors selling watermelons, apples, and loads of other fruits and vegetables from makeshift huts or directly out of their vehicles. I was surprised to see such variety considering their short growing season. I didn't know if these were locally grown or imported from elsewhere. We were offered a taste of watermelon, which was sweet and delicious, reminding me of home. One of the vendors wanted a photo with us, which we thought was interesting since we were usually the ones asking for them. We were happy to oblige.

The children of Khovd found us to be a curiosity. A group of ten kids emerged from nowhere to meet the American strangers. They ranged from about 8 to 12 years of age, dressed like kids of the same age in the US. Some of their clothing had English words, or trademarks like the Nike swoosh or Audi logo. I wondered if they knew the meaning behind them. They all knew a little English though only a few were conversational. Their curious questions included where we were from and where we were going. They were all polite, happy to take pictures with us, and eager to practice their English.

Cows and other animals frequently roamed around the city going wherever they liked. I thought that was fine, but it did lead to one other issue - there were piles of poop everywhere! Even though Khovd was large enough to have a few paved streets and pavestone sidewalks, you still had to be careful where you walked. Large animals leave huge piles that are not hard to miss as long as you were paying attention.

The evening brought us back to the hotel, and a taste of luxurious living. The Steppe Hotel was a modern five-story hotel, as nice as any hotel in the world. There was a great restaurant on the top floor with an outside patio overlooking the city. We finished the evening with a delicious meal at the hotel restaurant, a cold Mongolian beer, and a hot shower - the first one since the cabin in Tosontsengel. With a call home and a comfortable bed, life was good!

SEPTEMBER 17: BIKING DAY 23 – KHOVD – 0 BIKING MILES (476.5 BIKING MILES TOTAL) 0 RIDE MILES (1098.5 TOTAL MILES)

We had an enjoyable morning walk around the city of Khovd. I finally had the chance to exercise leg muscles other than my thighs. We walked (carefully avoiding cow pies) along the yellow and red pavestone sidewalks that extended through most of the city, past restaurants, shops, and houses. There was an amusement park with a Ferris wheel that was either closed for the season or closed for good. It looked like there had not been any activity for quite some time. It was sad to see the locked gates, and I imagined a time when the park was full of happy kids running around and having a good time.

Just beyond the amusement park was the Gandan Puntsag Choilon Khiid Monastery, the largest one in western Mongolia. It was similar to other monasteries, with an outer wall surrounding a courtyard and temples, but still unique and individual. The main gate led to a walkway lined with prayer wheels on each side. In the center of the courtyard was a familiar statue of the elephant, monkey, rabbit, and bird, in a dry fountain. Prayer benches for kneeling were in front of the statue. Along the top of the surrounding wall were dozens of stupas, or "mini temples," that I could walk by and view. Each stupa had a window revealing various items inside, like beads, holy relics, Buddha statues, or pictures of monks. This was an active monastery with ten monks living and working on site.

Behind the courtyard elephant statue was a yellow two-story temple where the strong smell of incense hit you as you walked through the door into a brightly colored room. The gray granite floor was about the only thing not painted in some intricate design. A picture of the Dalai Lama was proudly displayed between two large Buddhas along the back wall. There were smaller Buddha statues on the right and left walls, encased in blue cabinets behind glass. In the center were two rows of prayer benches on each side, red with gold trim, just like in the other temples. I could imagine the room filled with all ten monks chanting. The walls beneath the cabinets were also red with intricate gold trim, while the ceiling tiles were black with gold trim. Throughout the room were splashes of blue, white, red, green, and yellow - the colors of prayer flags.

On the left side of the room a monk in a red robe was seated at a table opposite two adult women, perhaps a mother and her daughter. The older woman was dressed in a traditional, full-length blue coat with green dots and white sash for a belt. Her gray hair poked out beneath her blue cap. The younger woman was in more Western clothing - a green T-shirt and black pants. Her black hair was pulled back in a short ponytail. There was a thin plume of smoke coming from a bowl of burning incense on the table. The only sound was the monk chanting in a continuous, low baritone voice, only pausing for a moment to breathe before continuing. As the monk chanted, the younger woman passed the burning incense around her body three times. Although I did not know what this blessing or prayer was about, it was fascinating to witness.

We proceeded to a second more modern-looking two-story building, also yellow with a red terracotta roof. The wooden double doors had elegant carvings along the outer edges. They were locked, so I assumed the monks lived there. Next to it was an impressive statue of Jhado Tulku, the "Abbot Emeritus" of the Namgyal Monastery. Located in India, the Namgyal Monastery is the personal monastery of the Dalai Lama, who is the leader of the Gelug school of Tibetan Buddhism. Jhado Tulku is one of the most highly esteemed lamas in the Gelug lineage. The beautiful statue conveyed great reverence. One needs to walk up two small flights of steps to approach the pedestal, which is raised another four feet. Jhado Tulku was 15 feet tall, seated on a high-backed throne with his arms crossed. I learned that sitting Buddhas represent teaching, meditation, or an attempt to reach enlightenment.

Other monuments with unusual shapes were on the grounds. I was sure they were deeply symbolic. There were a few monks in colorful robes strolling the grounds. Unfortunately, they disappeared before I was close enough to ask any questions, assuming they spoke English. Those hallowed temple grounds had been there for centuries, while outside the monastery walls there were billboards and high-rise buildings. I was struck by the clash of old meeting new.

Later in the afternoon, we stopped by a small but well-stocked market to top off our food supplies for the next segment of rural biking. In the market a woman overheard Jon and I talking and approached us speaking broken English. She introduced herself as Backutgood, saying she was Kazakh and wanted to show us her hand-sewn tapestries, hats, and decorative items. Maybe it is my New Jersey origins, but I have always been skeptical about things like this. I hate to admit it, but my first thought was this is a scam, and it could be dangerous to follow her. But she seemed harmless enough and, since Jon was interested, I went along. She walked us several blocks to her apartment building, which looked like a 1950s Soviet-style construction, and she led us upstairs to her home.

The apartment was small but very clean and quite sufficient. The living room had hardwood floors and a large beige area rug with red Kazakh designs in a repeating maze-like pattern. There was beautifully patterned wallpaper throughout, with bookcases, framed family pictures, and a flat screen television. Colorful tapestries hung on the walls. Next to the only window was a small galley kitchen. A door was on the opposite side which led to a bedroom. On the shelf was an award her daughter had earned for excelling in English at school. Next to that was a mathematics award given to her son. Backutgood then made us chai tea and snacks of watermelon and Kazakh bread called "bausak." She was a wonderful hostess and, while we knew we were there to buy something, she was in no hurry to sell us anything. She seemed more interested in conversation and perhaps a little English practice.

A short time later, Backutgood's three children came home from school - an older daughter and two sons. The younger ones appeared to be in grade school. The daughter was named Berikgoul, but everyone called her "Bailey." She was in 11th grade and spoke perfect American English while wearing a Brooklyn NY T-shirt. There were no pauses to find the right word or any hint of a Mongolian accent. She said her goal after graduating high school was to study economics either in Australia or the United States.

It was then that Backutgood brought out her bags of goods to show us. Bailey helped translate for her mother and explain each piece. There were beautiful tapestries of all colors, purses, hats, pants, potholders, a fox skin vest, and other similar items. We were traveling by bike with limited storage space, but it was difficult to pass up this chance to purchase such beautiful items. I bought two Kazakh hats, one for me and one for my son, because I knew he didn't have one. Jon had been looking for artwork or wall decorations. He bought a small tapestry that Backutgood said was over 60 years old. For a chance encounter in a market, the opportunity to meet this Kazakh family was beneficial for all of us. Backutgood sold her beautiful wares, Jon and I purchased unique gifts, and we shared time with an impressive family. As we parted, Bailey told Jon about a college in Indiana that she was interested in attending. Jon knew the college well and we agreed to exchange contact information. I was hopeful Jon or I could be of some help to this charming family.

Our next stop was the Hype Coffee Shop for a milkshake and piece of cake. I stayed away from the coffee and wondered if espressos were the reason for the name. I had been craving cake since visiting the bakery in Altai. I regretted not having eaten the luscious goodies in Altai, and I felt it was a missed opportunity. My mouth watered just thinking about those beautiful works of art emerging from cake heaven behind that little window! The cake at Hype was OK, but I believed the cake from the Altai bakery would have been better.

We returned to the hotel and began a conversation with Janah, who worked at the front desk in the lobby. Janah was a husky young man who looked to be in his late 20s. We thought he might be a good resource for local information. Weather and road conditions were important because the Altai Mountains had some steep peaks between us and the next town of Tolbo. There were no other towns or cultural sites along the way so, if we had problems, help would not be available. Janah's information confirmed what we had thought: wet weather and ice were likely in higher elevations. Under less-than-ideal conditions, our 3–4-day bike ride would be longer and riskier high up in the mountains. Janah said that he would be willing to help us with a ride over the worst of it. That seemed like a reasonable solution, and we quickly accepted his offer.

That evening Jon and I had dinner in the hotel restaurant and met an interesting couple from the UK, now living in France. Julie was a retired attorney, and Simon was a university professor doing research for a book about the successful reintroduction of the Takhi horse to Mongolia. Also called the Przewalski horse, this wild Mongolian breed was nearly extinct by 1960 with the few remaining ones living in zoos. They were smaller but stockier than most domestic horses, with adults weighing about 660 lbs. This breed was most likely the type of horse used by Chinggis Khaan and his warriors centuries ago. Mongolians take pride in the Takhi horse as a symbol of freedom and the spirit of the wild. French researchers had led a breeding program which helped their numbers to increase. A small herd was released in the French mountains, and the horses thrived. Given this success, horses were then brought to Mongolia and released. Now several hundred Takhi horses are thought to roam the grasslands of their ancestral home. Simon was there to document the status of the horses, and his forthcoming book will highlight the success of this conservation effort.

SEPTEMBER 18: BIKING DAY 24 – KHOVD TO TOLBO – 7.0 BIKING MILES (483.5 BIKING MILES TOTAL) 94.4 RIDE MILES (1192.9 TOTAL MILES)

We had agreed to meet Janah at 10:00 in the morning and, right on time, he was there. He looked comfortable in the cool weather wearing two T-shirts, black jeans, and a billed cap. Janah had experience packing his small car. A cargo rack the size of his car roof made it easy to strap down the bikes securely.

We had an enjoyable ride through some interesting terrain. Initially it looked like a desert with dry, sandy soil and brown clumps of dead vegetation. There were no herds or grazing livestock in this area. The road kept to the open, flat areas most of the time but there was a noticeable climb in elevation as we drove toward the snowcapped mountains. The dark, ominous clouds hovering over the mountains gave off a foreboding feeling. As the elevation increased, grass reappeared with the return of grazing animals. A group of yaks took over the road, and we had to wait for their permission to proceed. Two yaks stood in our way, staring at us through the windshield. They seemed to know that they were in charge and only allowed us to go when the rest of their small herd moved away.

The steep climb continued until Janah made a stop for a view atop one of the high mountain passes. We stepped out of the warm car into the snow, gusting winds and sub-freezing temperatures. We enjoyed seeing the snow-covered mountains all around us, but the frigid temperatures quickly drove us back into the car. The bitterly cold conditions confirmed we had made the right decision to get a ride rather than trying to pedal through terrain like this. It would be insane to even think about biking through these mountains. Jon's altimeter peaked at 8,750 feet, which was about 4,000 feet higher than our starting point in Khovd, and about 3,500 feet higher than Denver, CO!

The road passed through the "town" of Hongo, which was only a town because it was named on a map. In reality, it looked like two former businesses, both now closed, and three structures which may have been houses, all now empty. I would say the population of Hongo was zero. Further down the road was another point on the map called Bayan-Engel which, like Hongo, may have had people living there at one time but not anymore. Our goal for the day was Tolbo, and we were told it was a thriving town. I sure hoped it had more to offer than Hongo and Bayan-Engel.

Janah drove down the paved primary road for another hour or more until stopping at a sign marking the left turn to Tolbo. There was a small village several miles down a dirt road, which Janah said was Tolbo. He drove us to the town where the dirt road doubled as their one busy main street. There were several shops lining both sides of the street, with housing behind. I was slightly disappointed to find no hotels in Tolbo, but there was a restaurant. Since we were currently at a much lower elevation, the expected nighttime temperature of 40°F would be tolerable in tents. We returned to the paved road and found an area near the Tolbo sign to make a campsite, with an outhouse nearby and cattle grazing on the dry, mostly yellow grass beyond. It did not take long to unload Janah's car. The tents went up, the air mattresses were inflated, and the sleeping bags rolled out. It was better to have done that now than later in the evening when the temperatures dropped.

With our home for the night set up, we biked down the dirt road back to the restaurant in Tolbo. The restaurant was empty, with only a serious-looking older woman with gray hair in the kitchen and a smiling ten-year-old girl who may have been her granddaughter. The kitchen looked spotless and well stocked. The woman brought out menus, and we pointed to what we wanted.

We had just ordered dinner when three men came in, one of them obviously drunk. The drunk man was probably in his mid-50s while his two friends were older, maybe in their 60s, all wearing black pants and black leather jackets. Their faces appeared 'weather worn' but maybe it was just a hard day. The drunk one immediately struck up a conversation with us, thinking we were Russian. We told him "No, Americans" and he nodded in agreement. He identified himself as Makey and was proud to say he was Kazakh rather than Mongolian. I was unaware of any tension between Kazakhs and Mongolians, but apparently Makey had a preference. The farther west one goes in Mongolia, the more ethnically diverse it becomes. Russia and China meet along the Mongolian border, and Kazakhstan lies just a little farther to the west. Makey wanted to "friend" me on Facebook and asked me to pull up my account, but thankfully there was no internet service. Since I don't speak Kazakh, and Makey didn't speak English, I doubted being "friends" would have been successful anyway.

After Makey and his friends finished their meal, he decided to join our table for a few photos. Makey squeezed in next to me and all the phones came out for pictures. I tried not to get too close to avoid the alcohol smell on his breath. Things went well until a vodka bottle fell out of his coat pocket. The woman who ran the restaurant stormed out of the kitchen with heated words for Makey. She apparently did not tolerate alcohol in her establishment. Makey must have known he was in trouble and put up no resistance. Without knowing the words, I knew exactly what she was saying as she threw Makey and his friends out of her restaurant.

We finished our meal in peace and then roamed around Tolbo. The main street along the storefronts had a short section of paved road, while all the residential streets behind it were dirt. Looking down one road, I saw smoke drifting up from several stovepipes. Many of the houses were behind walls of rock or cinder blocks. The homes were a mixture of wood, brick, or cinder block construction. There were several gers (although Kazakhs call them "yurts") and a few shacks with corrugated metal roofs. Outside the houses there were piles of animal dung 3-4 feet high, carefully spread out to dry. This would be used as fuel for their stoves in winter. One specific dung pile caught my eye. Looking over the wall, I saw dozens of tall towers made from dung, carefully arranged with smaller pieces stacked atop larger ones to form thin pyramids. Busy in the backyard was a 12-year-old boy who introduced himself as Akmed, carefully sorting out the animal dung to dry. He was something of an artisan in the world of dung statues, and I was impressed with his talent. Most of his creations were over two feet tall. We said "hello," and he said "hi," but he was much too busy for an extended conversation. Akmed allowed us to take a few pictures, but then we left him to do his chores.

We found that while Mongolians were primarily Buddhist, most Kazakhs were Muslim. We saw a small mosque in the center of town with a crescent sitting over a blue-domed roof. A small minaret was in the opposite corner. Val and I had visited a large mosque in Turkey the previous year, with a large open central prayer hall for the men's prayer mats and a smaller section off to the side for women. I was curious how this one would compare. Unfortunately, the building was closed, and we were unable to see inside the prayer hall.

Our updated weather forecast said nighttime temperatures might approach freezing, so it was time to layer up and get into my warm sleeping bag. It was only 6:30, but it felt like time to call it a day. Since we had no internet, and no way to call home, sleep seemed like the best option. I always felt disappointed when I was unable to contact home. Jon and I were in very remote areas for most of the trip. I thought about what Val and the kids might be doing and what they might be thinking when they didn't hear from me.

With a one-man tent, there was limited room. The shoes and backpack stayed outside under the rain flap. Weather determined what my "pajamas" were, as in how many layers to wear. My 20-degree sleeping bag with fleece liner kept me warm enough in above freezing temperatures. Below freezing, I added an extra layer of clothes and wool socks. I liked putting the next day's clothes in the sleeping bag with me. That way they were warm in the morning and easily available if I needed another layer in the middle of a really cold night. As I took one last look at the mountains, I saw a misty rain falling over one of the nearby peaks. Even though we had limited weather information for the mountains, I was pretty sure we would have a dry night. About an hour later, I heard a soft rain hitting my tent. Oh well - at least inside the tent was warm and dry.

SEPTEMBER 19: BIKING DAY 25 – TOLBO TO TOLBO LAKE RESORT – 20.0 BIKING MILES (503.5 BIKING MILES TOTAL) 0 RIDE MILES (1212.9 TOTAL MILES)

I woke up early in the morning to find a thin layer of ice on my tent. Since we had no specific schedule, and a relatively short biking day of paved roads and mostly flat terrain ahead, there was no urgent need to get out of my warm sleeping bag. Around 7:30 I heard Jon in his tent, and he said it was 28°F. This was lower than we expected, which was not surprising in the mountains. I laid in my sleeping bag for another hour watching the ice melt and drip down the outside of the tent as the sun rose. It sure would have been nice if Val had been there with me in that small little tent. Sweet snuggles are wonderful, and something I missed. Over the years we have had plenty of tent camping adventures, even with our kids and dogs. I knew we would have more, but maybe not anytime soon. I would be happy just to be back on our deck again, watching the sunset with a glass of wine.

Gradually, the temperatures crept above freezing and we began our day. I now had time to reflect on our trip to this point. The early thoughts of "will we make it?" were no longer a concern. Ulgii was only 50 miles away, which could be done in one long day of biking. The house in Ulgii that Jon had arranged would not be available for a few days. The car ride through the desert had put us ahead of schedule, which allowed us plenty of time to relax. Relaxation seemed like a welcome gift! My thoughts turned to reaching Ulgii, and the fun trip through the Altai Mountains followed by the Eagle Festival. In just over two weeks we would begin our journey home.

After the usual breakfast of tea and oatmeal with raisins, we began to pack up for another biking day. It was a good day, with cool temperatures and no rain. After a few miles, we came upon Tolbo Nuur. "Nuur" is the Mongolian word for lake. It is a picturesque body of clear blue water nestled against the backdrop of snowcapped mountains. The lake was about twenty miles long, so we enjoyed beautiful scenery for most of the day. A large group of yaks dotted the landscape along with a small herd of wild horses.

We came upon a car parked by the side of the road with two people enjoying the view. We stopped briefly to speak with the couple, who were from Amsterdam. They had just come from Ulgii and remarked on what a great time they had and how much they enjoyed the people there. Ulgii is large enough to offer a variety of good restaurants, markets, and just about everything someone could want. They were on their way to Ulaanbaatar, which made me think of how close we were to Ulgii and how far they still had to go. We had left over three weeks ago, which seemed like the distant past. Of course, driving is a lot faster than biking, but they were still days away. We warned them about the horrible dirt road between Altai and Uliastai. I hoped their car was sturdy.

After a somewhat challenging 1.5-mile climb, we arrived at the Tolbo Lake Resort, located at the edge of the lake with a long, rocky dirt road leading to it. A road like this had already broken my cargo rack, but the makeshift repair of duct tape and cable ties seemed to be holding up. I had to carefully pick my way around rocks and ruts that could ruin my repair work.

On arrival, we met Botkild and Sosan, a husband-and-wife team who managed the resort. I was happy to see them, as the place otherwise looked deserted. Botkild led us to our log cabin, which was large and modern. It looked like it was recently constructed, with wood rafters, log walls, and heated hardwood floors. We each had two beds - one for sleeping and one to spread out our gear. Everything was spotlessly clean. Our next stop was the bathhouse, which had shower stalls and a hot water heater. This truly was a resort! Being the off-season, their cabins, yurts, playground, basketball court, and floating dock at the small beach were all vacant. There was also a large banquet hall, complete with a mirrored ceiling ball, just waiting for the next wedding.

It was now time for lunch, and Sosan prepared a much-appreciated hot meal for us. I had cuivan (also spelled tsuivan), which is a traditional Mongolian dish of meat, noodle, and vegetables, along with soup and milk tea. It was delicious and very filling. We ate in the large banquet hall located next to the kitchen. I tried to ask Sosan how many weddings they have had there, but my question was lost in translation. My guess was that there were many. I also wanted to know about Sosan's kitchen, which she was pleased to show me. She smiled when I motioned if I could take a picture. It was clean and modern with stainless-steel tables and two gas stoves on a spotless floor. A large wok sat next to a few pots on top of the burners. I could imagine how busy this kitchen must be during one of their big events.

Sosan's kitchen

My next order of business was a hot shower - a rare treat, but oh so necessary. The wind was kicking up outside, and a chill was in the air, making a hot shower all the more welcome. Even though the temperatures were cool, biking had left me sweaty. With the last shower 2-3 days ago, and no recent laundry, it was likely that our clothes smelled worse than we did. The bathhouse had a restroom with tiled walls and a metal partition creating two shower stalls. One stall had warm water and the other had hot, so it was worth waiting for the "good" shower with hot water.

We were now just 30 miles from our final destination of Ulgii. Riding bikes, we could be there in a day, but the availability for our rental house was not ready yet. With the extra time, we thought the best option was to stay at the lake resort and enjoy all it had to offer. Our extended stay allowed plenty of time to wash clothes and enjoy the scenery. There was a small store that was well-stocked with alcohol. We treated ourselves to a bottle of red wine and cookies. Although the wine was not great, I liked the idea of having it. Feeling triumphant, it seemed like a good time to celebrate our accomplishments to this point.

The day ended with my usual routine of brushing my teeth and the nighttime trip to the outhouse before going to bed. As I left the cabin and walked into the darkness, I could see about twenty pairs of eerie, glowing eyes staring back at me in the light of my headlamp, blocking my way to the bathhouse. Knowing they were not people, I stopped and wondered what kind of creatures they might be. My mind raced through a quick threat assessment, trying to remember what types of predators might be here. Mongolia does have wolves, but they should be in the northern mountains closer to the Russian border. Maybe a pack of wild dogs, but the eyes seemed too big for dogs. Goats? Sheep? After a few moments my eyes adjusted, and I made out a small group of cows wandering around eating grass. They were completely harmless, only pausing briefly as I interrupted their late-night snack. Feeling relieved, I went on my way, and they went on theirs.

Just as I was drifting off to sleep, the sound of a party began. I couldn't make out the language, but the laughter and music came through loud and clear. Apparently, we were not the only ones staying at the resort. If it had been warmer outside, I might have joined them for a beer, but I was content to stay in my warm bed and sleep. I thought the noise would fade away soon enough, but these hearty partiers had stamina. The noise and music continued until about 4 a.m. I was not sure if the party ended or if I just fell asleep in spite of it. Either way, they had fun, and I eventually got some rest.

SEPTEMBER 20: BIKING DAY 26 – TOLBO LAKE RESORT – 0 BIKING MILES (503.5 BIKING MILES TOTAL) 0 RIDE MILES (1212.9 TOTAL MILES)

This was a day off to enjoy the Tolbo Lake Resort. After walking along the edge of the water and climbing a small hill for a better view of the lake, my chore list for the day was completed. It was a rare treat to have a day with nothing to do. Tolbo Lake was a picturesque setting and home for a flock of geese. The beautiful blue water and surrounding mountains blanketed with snow made me feel like I was in the Swiss Alps!

Tolbo Lake at sunset

At midday, the loud party crowd from last night began to wake up and wander around. They were Asian, in their young 20s, perhaps more Korean than Mongolian. I nodded hello to some of them, but we had a language barrier, and they didn't seem interested in having a chat.

Although it was a beautiful sunny day with T-shirt temperatures, there wasn't much to do. Naps took care of the early afternoon. I thought we had earned them, but Jon did not have the time to nap.

During the trip, he and his wife were selling their house in Indiana and buying a new one in Pennsylvania. There were countless emails and many phone calls made during the morning and evening hours involving realtors, inspectors, and contractors. Buying and selling a house is a daunting task under the best of circumstances, but this was quite a feat on different continents over 6,000 miles apart! I thought it was most difficult for his wife, who was tasked with the daily details along with the responsibility of finding a new home. Jon would not even see his new house until after closing. But, as Jon explained, the Mongolia trip was planned well before the decision to move occurred. It was just unfortunate for them both that the house transactions happened to be at this particular time.

In the mid-afternoon, our hostess Sosan woke me up to ask about the evening meal. With my translator in hand, I pointed to several items on the menu which she said were not available. We compromised on the same meal I had last night. It may have been the only food she had left. I had no complaints, as Sosan made tasty food in healthy proportions that was quite satisfying.

The attempt to split the room and restaurant bill between Jon and I was a failure. The credit card machine in the restaurant only had enough charge for one transaction. None of my three credit cards would work due to "low battery" on the machine. Jon and I pooled our money and had just enough cash to cover everything we owed at the resort. We would be camping tomorrow and wouldn't need cash until we reached Ulgii, which was sure to have plenty of ATMs.

After returning to our cabin, we left the door open in the hope that the flies would leave. Three young men approached and knocked on the door. I assumed they were part of the party crowd that kept us up last night. They were speaking in what sounded like Korean, but I didn't know for sure. They seemed a bit stressed and somewhat insistent, which made me suspicious. Since we were speaking in different languages, things came to a standstill. I motioned if they had a translator on their phone, which they did. One of them quickly typed, then showed me the English translation: "toilet paper." I now understood why they were so insistent. I shared my roll of toilet paper and they quickly left. This was a lesson I learned early on. Most places do not have toilet paper, so it is important to have your own.

SEPTEMBER 21: BIKING DAY 27 – TOLBO LAKE RESORT – 0 BIKING MILES (503.5 BIKING MILES TOTAL) 0 RIDE MILES (1212.9 TOTAL MILES)

The beautifully clear, star-filled night sky turned into a cold, wet, windy, gray, miserable morning. A nearby flagpole with the Mongolian flag was blowing completely horizontal by the strong wind. I could look out the cabin window and see whitecaps on the lake. The amount of snow on the mountaintops had increased since the previous day.

It was difficult to obtain accurate weather forecasts in our remote location. We were at 7,300 feet elevation and the weather apps we had were not reliable. Just as my weather app indicated there was not going to be rain for another six hours, I heard the rain hitting the roof of our cabin. Apparently, there was a cold front coming up from China bringing bad weather. This would make for a rough day biking. The front should pass in 24 hours and hopefully leave sunny weather behind it. The worst-case scenario was to stay at the resort for an extra day and then bike to Ulgii when the weather improved. It wasn't a difficult decision. With better weather expected soon, and being super motivated to reach our final destination, the last day of biking should be easy.

Jon cooked eggs and made me an egg tortilla for breakfast. It was a step above my usual oatmeal. It rained most of the day, so Jon worked on his laptop while I played solitaire and took naps. There were times before I retired from my job where I just wanted a day with nothing to do and nothing on my schedule. My wish had come true. I only wished Google would update its news feeds more frequently as I read and reread the same stories. The flies kept me amused, buzzing around the cabin. No matter how many I swatted, there were always 4 or 5 more flying around.

By midafternoon the rain slowed, and I could see the mountains on the other side of the lake again. The clouds began to break up, with small bits of blue sky peeking through. September was reportedly the dry season in Mongolia, with only a fraction of an inch of rain for the month. Maybe that was true in the desert, but not in the mountains. It rained for nearly the entire day.

Botkild finally charged his credit card machine, which meant we could enjoy one more of Sosan's dinners. It was the same food as before, but I had become accustomed to noodles and mutton. It seemed to be the meal of choice in every restaurant.

As I crawled into bed, not very tired from all the napping, I could hear rain starting to hit the metal cabin roof again, each drop landing with a sharp *thwack*. I was grateful not to be in a tent. We hoped tomorrow would be a better day to get back on the bikes.

SEPTEMBER 22: BIKING DAY 28 – TOLBO LAKE RESORT TO ULGII – 29.7 BIKING MILES (533.2 BIKING MILES TOTAL) 0 RIDE MILES (1242.6 TOTAL MILES)

I woke up to a chilly, partly cloudy sky with temperatures just below freezing, but at least it was dry. The good news was that the dark clouds were behind us, with patches of blue sky ahead.

As I was packing my bike, a tall, thin man in his early 20s approached and introduced himself. Alex was a Russian man in Mongolia on holiday. He was evasive when I asked him more about his travels, saying only that he was headed to Ulaanbaatar. He appeared to be traveling alone. I explained that I was from the US, and we had a polite conversation about our travels. He seemed to be planning an extended stay in Mongolia and was not overly eager to get back to Russia. I wondered if being a military-aged male had something to do with that. I deeply wished we could talk about politics but did not feel it was appropriate. We wished each other safe travels as he walked to his SUV, then he headed east towards Ulaanbaatar. As his vehicle disappeared into a cloud of dust down the dirt road, I thought about his situation. With the ongoing war in Ukraine, there were countless people like Alex on both sides who would continue to be killed. If Alex returned to Russia, he would probably end up in a military unit in Ukraine. For his sake, I hoped he stayed in Mongolia.

My bike was finally packed, Jon was ready, and our journey was nearly complete. This was the last day of biking! There was a wide-open swath of land between us and the main paved road, with scattered dirt paths leading in different directions. To avoid the brutal washboard road from our arrival, we took a chance on a smoother-looking dirt track toward the main paved road. I hoped that my repaired cargo rack would fare better on a smoother path. The road we took connected to a second dirt road, which connected to a third, each one becoming a bit less like a road and more like an open prairie. It took a great amount of effort to pedal through the soft, granular soil. Eventually, we discovered a "good" dirt road leading to the main road. Our little side trip did not save us any time, but it was a little less jarring on the bikes - and on us as well.

Once we made it back to the main road, it was an easy ride. The paved road had a few small hills but was mostly flat and free of potholes. At the top of one hill, we saw a small white cinder block building that appeared to be a store, with a sign over the door written in several different languages. I recognized "Galerie D'Art" and "Café" on the sign. We entered and met Jan and his wife. They not only ran the store but also lived there. Jan spoke English and said he was originally from Switzerland but moved here with his Mongolian wife. Their humble store included a small bedroom, with its walls made from grain sacks. The rest of the building had shelves with food and other items, some for sale and some for their own use. While we were taking in our charming surroundings, two shivering Mongolian men arrived on a motorcycle. Jan's wife hurried to make them hot tea. We were also offered tea but declined, eager to continue on to our goal of Ulgii. As we pedaled away, I wondered why they chose to live a solitary life in such an extremely remote area. I could understand "getting away from it all," but I don't think I have that kind of commitment in me. The world is filled with amazing people.

Jon and his bike outside the "country store"

The miles clicked away, and we grew closer to Ulgii with every turn of the pedal. I watched the km markers on the side of the road, counting down the distance. As we crested our final hill climb of the trip, I could see a lengthy downhill road leading to a city in the distance – Ulgii. It was still 7 km away, but our goal was in sight.

When we were close to the city, we stopped to take selfies at the "I Heart Ulgii" sign. There was another sign farther down the road that also made a great photo opportunity. As we struggled to capture the sign, both bikes, and ourselves in the same image, a friendly voice asked if he could take the picture for us. It was Julie and Simon, the friends we had met from the Steppe Hotel in Khovd a few days earlier. Simon had completed his research on the Przewalski horses, and they were on their way to the airport in Ulgii to head back to Ulaanbaatar. They were driving by and just happened to see us - what an amazing coincidence, with perfect timing to the second! They took our pictures along with a few group shots. Simon said they were very successful in finding and documenting the healthy status of the horses, "beyond all expectations!" We traded contact information, and I hoped to hear from them when Simon's book was published.

We entered Ulgii early that afternoon and were greeted by dozens of young children walking home from school. Just about everyone smiled, waved, and practiced their "hellos" to us. We obviously stood out as foreigners, and the smiles and greetings felt very welcoming. Ulgii is the second largest city in western Mongolia, with a population of almost 30,000, behind Ulaangom, with a population of 38,000. Kazakhstan lies just west of Mongolia, and the two countries are separated by the 62-mile Russian-Chinese border. Western Mongolia has a strong Kazakh influence from the migration of its people out of Kazakhstan over the past two centuries - first fleeing the growing control of Tsar Nicholas II's Imperial Russian Empire, then the Bolsheviks after the Russian Revolution of 1917, and later the communists and Soviet Russia. Ulgii was the Mongolian center of Islam before Stalin's religious purges in the 1930s destroyed the mosques and its leaders, just as was done to Buddhists during the same time period. Today the mosques have been rebuilt, and people are free to practice whatever religion they wish. Kazakhs are the largest ethnic minority in Mongolia, comprising 3-4% of the total population, and they actually outnumber Mongolians in the far western regions of the country.

Jon had arranged an Airbnb with Boka from Maral Expeditions, a tour group based in Ulgii. Boka had an empty three-bedroom house available for the remainder of our stay. Boka used this house in the summer for his tour business, then traveled to Ulaanbaatar to live in his "winter house" for the off-season. Our car ride across the Gobi Desert had saved us time and allowed us to arrive in Ulgii a few days early. Since we had extra time, Boka had offered us a four-day tour through the Kazakh areas of western Mongolia, which sounded both fun and educational. I was looking forward to sightseeing without having to pedal there.

When we arrived at Boka's house, a young woman was waiting for us. Bota (Boka's sister) showed us the house, which had one bedroom. The other two "bedrooms" were used as office space for Maral Expeditions and full of desks and boxes. Bota showed me the living room with my bed (the sofa) next to a desk, with a sheet and blanket on top. It was just a sofa - not even a sofa bed - but it would have to do. I was finally in Ulgii and not in a tent, so I was satisfied. To be truthful, camping in a tent was not all that bad. I was always dry inside, comfortable on the air mattress, and warm in my cozy sleeping bag. I just didn't like getting out in the morning, especially if it was cold and wet. But given the choice between a tent and a bed, I'd take the bed.

Ulgii, the finish line!

Downtown Ulgii with a Russian van passing by

Ulgii seemed cosmopolitan by Mongolian standards. The main streets were paved, the sidewalks were in good shape, and the buildings ranged from old to new. We explored Ulgii on foot, which was a welcome change from biking. A short walk from our house was a central square, consisting of a city-block-sized plaza. In the center was a large statue of a war hero on horseback, his cape trailing behind. The statue memorializes "The Hero of Mongolia" Ekei Mazim, known as the "Fierce Eagle of Altai." In 1939, the Japanese Imperial Army encroached on Mongolian territory. A fierce battle ensued, where combined Russian-Mongolian forces defeated the Japanese. Although mortally wounded, Ekei Mazim continued to lead his troops until the end.

Surrounding the plaza were numerous restaurants, souvenir shops, and other businesses. At one end stood a government office building with the Mongolian flag proudly fluttering in the light breeze. On the opposite side, a block or two off the plaza, was the black market. Unfortunately, it was closed, but at least we knew where it was. Like the one in Ulaanbaatar, there were many small booths lining the maze of improvised alleys created by the shopkeepers. I knew there were bargains to be found during their hours of operation. I felt reassured that black markets are no longer the seedy, nefarious places of decades past. They were legitimate businesses that still allowed a little negotiation of prices. The Ulgii market was smaller than the one in Ulaanbaatar but looked like a good place for unique shopping ideas.

Walking around the streets near the central plaza, we saw posters for a circus that weekend. That sounded like fun - how could we pass up an opportunity like that? We made a point to get tickets for the following day. Dinner that night was at a quaint little coffee shop with good food and a pleasant atmosphere. Jon had a knack for finding interesting little cafes. It was up one flight of stairs, where we entered a large room with tables on one side and a counter along the opposite wall. The menu was limited but better than expected with several items other than meat and noodles. After dinner we had a leisurely walk back to the house for a hot shower and a comfortable sofa.

Back at the house, I noticed a bookcase along the wall. One book I enjoyed thumbing through was "How to Speak English" written for Mongolians. It was far more comprehensive than I expected. Those who studied from that book would probably speak better English than I do. Of course, that is not that big a stretch compared to someone with 'Jersey roots who still says "dowg" instead of "dog."

I unpacked my bags and spread everything out, eager to separate things I no longer needed, like the tent, camp stove, etc. We had finally made it to Ulgii, our finish line. The biking was over. I had a feeling of great relief having accomplished our goal, and anticipated boarding a plane back home in just over a week. We had traveled a long way, challenging ourselves both physically and mentally. This had been an amazing adventure, and it was not yet over. In thirty years of marriage, I had never been apart from my wife for more than a few days at a time. I really missed her. I felt lucky to have had fairly frequent phone calls, but it was not the same. I kept imagining her 'welcome home' hug at the airport. I just had to hang on for twelve more days...

SEPTEMBER 23: ULGII

A day of leisure with no biking! I was in a reflective mood that morning, thinking about the past several weeks. I had felt a sense of freedom on the open road, taking in the beautiful scenery. Having all day to bike thirty miles was not difficult if the roads were reasonable. There were days when my thighs hurt from the steep mountains, but I felt lucky that we had no significant problems along the way. We stayed in nice hotels, horrible hotels, gers, and tents. It was, at times, uncomfortably hot, freezing cold, then wet and cold as we biked through hail and thunderstorms. Overall, it was an amazing experience, meeting awesome people and seeing a way of life unlike what I was used to. I was fortunate to have experienced it!

Ulgii was large enough to have paved streets and traffic, something that was oddly comforting to see again. After walking through the central square, we arrived at a black market. If I needed shoes, I would be in luck. There were loads of people selling them, with everything from bedroom slippers to steel-toed work boots. Some had women's shoes and high heels, while others sold shoes for children of all ages. Most of the other items in the market were basic necessities such as clothing, jackets, household goods and essential things like that. One woman was selling dombras, a traditional musical instrument resembling a small guitar with a long neck and only two strings. The strings are plucked or strummed to produce a melodic sound. Dombras are found throughout Mongolia and Central Asia and are an important part of the region's cultural heritage.

I had been looking for exotic, unusual Christmas gifts and was not disappointed. I bought a few things at the black market, and the retail shops around the center square took care of the rest. Mongolia is the world's leading producer of cashmere, accounting for roughly half of the world's supply. It is harvested in the spring, when cashmere goats naturally shed their soft undercoat. The desired fiber is the soft down, which must be separated from the coarse hair. While it can be sheared, the finest fibers are collected by hand with a comb, which causes no harm to the animal. This is used to create incredibly soft yet warm material for clothing and other items. I bought hats, scarves, and a sweater for my wife and family, all at bargain prices compared to back home.

Kazakh embroidery is unique, being very detailed and colorful. I found lovely pillowcases and small purses unlike anything I had ever seen before. Of course, everyone was going to get Mongolian slippers for Christmas that year. The same type of slippers were found in every black market, often being sold by several different vendors. They seemed very popular, so I guess that meant something. Men's slippers, for my son and me, looked like boots with swirling designs on each side. Women's slippers, for my wife and daughter, were slip-on style. I bought one with a camel and one with a geometric pattern.

We continued to see posters advertising the circus in town. We bought tickets for the 3:00 show, allowing us time to shop and bring our bounty back to the house before the show began. When we returned to the arena for the circus, it was almost a mob scene. There were hundreds of people all trying to enter through a single open door. There was something of a line trying to form, but most people ignored that and pushed straight towards the door. All at once, the people in line started to become angry. Tempers flared, and the yelling began. We had no desire to be a part of the mob, but there was no escaping it. I was fascinated, but a little nervous, hearing people cuss at each other in Mongolian. I could have learned a few new words if I had been paying close enough attention. The poor man working the door was overwhelmed. All he could do was let people in as fast as he could to keep things moving.

After we were pushed through the door and inside the building, I felt safer. We found seats and waited for the show to begin. One difference between events here and at home is the lack of merchandise sales. I wanted to buy a circus poster or souvenir with Mongolian words for my daughter, a former acrobat and proud alumna of the Florida State University Flying High Circus. Without merchandise sales, I had to resort to taking a poster from the public billboard outside. Criminal charges seemed unlikely since this was the last day for the circus.

Soon the lights went up, the music played, and the ringmaster appeared. I didn't know if he was speaking Mongolian or Kazakh, but I understood the show was about to begin. He introduced act after act, with acrobats, jugglers, clowns, and feats of impressive strength, balance, and focus. I had as much fun seeing the amazed faces of the kids sitting around us as I did watching the show. There were animal acts with cats, dogs, peacocks, racoons, a porcupine, a snake, and an ostrich. Some acts did not go as planned, as one dog kept running off the stage for safety behind the curtains. One of the cats was to walk a narrow plank between two stools but found it easier to jump down and walk on the floor instead. When it comes to kids and animals, you never know what to expect. Overall, I thought the circus was great. All the performers had amazing talent. Who wouldn't be entertained by a woman pedaling a ten-foot unicycle playing a saxophone?

After the show, Jon found the Pamukkale Turkish Restaurant, which looked like a great spot for dinner. They had a menu in English and a variety of foods beyond the usual noodles and mutton we had become accustomed to. The generous menu offered choices of meatballs, shish kebabs, rolled grape leaves stuffed with meat and rice, dumplings, flatbreads, and pastries made with thin, flaky phyllo dough. The artwork on the walls depicted scenes from Istanbul, which I recognized from when Val and I visited there the year before. I felt lucky Jon found this gem of a restaurant.

After dinner, the weather began to turn cold. It seemed like a long walk back to our little rental house. While bundling up walking in the cold, I thought of our family ski vacations in Colorado. We would walk through the cold evening air along the main street of a small mountain town, with snowcapped peaks seeming to rise at the end of the street. Those vacations were years ago, but the walk tonight vividly brought it all back. I hoped someday there would be something to trigger this memory - walking around Ulgii on a cold evening after traveling across this huge country – and bring back many fond memories.

SEPTEMBER 24: ULGII

It was a cold, wet day. The weather app said it would be in the low 30s all day with 100% chance of precipitation later in the day and into the evening. Around midmorning, the first snow fell. It was a light dusting, but it was still snow. Jon went back to the black market while I had no reason to go out in the freezing cold. I stayed in the house where it was still cold, but a little bit warmer and drier than outside.

Our house was not exactly like it was described to us by Boka, the owner:

- Three bedrooms? Yes, but two of the bedrooms were offices for Boka's tour business and not accessible to us.
- Heat? Yes, but the coal-burning furnace spewed toxic fumes, so it was not used. Two small space heaters produced minimal heat for the entire house.
- Hot water? Yes, but using the hot pot with the space heaters blows the circuit breaker. We learned the hard way that the hot water heater must be manually reset every time the circuit breaker blows.
- Showers? Yes, but it is a handheld hose in the bathtub.
- Indoor plumbing? Yes, but without a toilet. The outhouse is in the yard.

While Jon was out, I had a visit from Boka's sister, Bota, and her interpreter. Bota was taking care of her brother's tour business while Boka and his family were at their winter home in Ulaanbaatar. We owed Boka money for our stay at his house and the four-day tour we were due to start the next day. The problem was they could not take a credit card; they would only accept cash. Even after my trip to the ATM yesterday, I was still $150 short. We would have to make another visit to the ATM. I explained that we were good for the money we owed them, but that was all the cash we had. We would pay them in full before we left. They seemed reluctant at first, but, since we did not have the money, they had no choice but to wait for us to pay the balance. I felt a little bad about this, but not enough to go out on a cold, wet day to find an ATM. I promised they would get their money, just not right now. Otherwise, it was a low-key day. My things were organized for our upcoming four-day adventure, so I could squeeze in a nap. My tasks for the day would then be completed!

Jon and I enjoyed the Turkish restaurant so much that we returned there for dinner, even though it was about a mile away. The walk seemed longer, thinking about which great meal I was going to have. The Turkish tea would be a beautiful compliment to the food.

While walking home after dinner, it began to snow again. The Colorado feeling returned, which helped me forget the cold. I suppose the warm jacket helped too. The daytime high temperatures in the 30s F would drop into the low 20s F at night. If the temperature inside the house stayed above freezing, I would be alright.

SEPTEMBER 25: TAVAN BOGD NATIONAL PARK

Today would begin our four-day excursion to the Altai Mountains near the western border of Mongolia. Boka put an itinerary together, including a guide and driver which sounded terrific:

- Day one we were scheduled to go to Tavan Bogd National Park and meet the ranger. We would have a day of hiking to a glacier and sightseeing in the mountains, then stay overnight in a yurt provided by the ranger.
- Day two we would spend with Kazakh shepherds to learn about their herd, discuss wool and cashmere production, and witness daily life in the mountains. We would stay in a yurt with the shepherds at night.
- Day three we would visit a ranch and ride horses to a beautiful waterfall deep in the mountains.
- Day four we would return to Ulgii.

All the food was to be provided, with "hearty breakfasts, mouthwatering dinners, and delicious snacks." My packing for the tour was easy since they were taking care of everything. We were told all we needed was our clothes. I could leave my food and first aid bag behind which lightened my load considerably.

At the designated time our guide, Ainep, and driver, Akbolat, arrived in "the Russian van." Imagine an old Soviet-era gray van. It was very basic, with a boxy design, old-fashioned round headlights, and no frills on the inside. These vans are all over Mongolia, particularly in the western areas. They were all identical, except for a few painted army green. They looked like Cold War relics seen in spy movies set in the 1950s. I was a little skeptical, concerned that it might break down in some desolate area, but since they are very commonly seen I rationalized they must be easy to repair.

Knowing that we would be out of internet and cell tower range, I sent my wife contact information with a picture of Boka's business card and a picture of the van with the "Maral Expeditions" logo, just in case she needed it. I didn't know why, I just had this feeling...

As we opened the van door to climb in, I was hit by the strong smell of gasoline. This did not ease my skeptical feeling. I didn't think that was normal, but what do I know? It was my first time in a Russian van. Jon and I sat in the back where there were no seatbelts. After Akbolat made a quick stop at a market for a bag of snacks, we were off to the mountains.

Ainep and Akbolat were both Kazakh. They were friendly, but only Ainep spoke English. Communications with Akbolat that did not go through Ainep were mostly nods and gestures. They acted like they had worked together in the past and seemed to make a good team. We quickly left downtown Ulgii, and our surroundings immediately became more rural.

We headed west and it did not take long before we ran out of paved road. The rest of the 180 km trip was on bumpy dirt roads. The roads were rough, and at times we were literally bouncing in our seats. Seatbelts would have helped. There were washboard roads, large rocks, steep grades, and water crossings, yet nothing stopped our Russian van. I admired both the van and the driver for safely getting us over the difficult terrain. The skill of our driver, Akbolat, was truly impressive. At times there was a spaghetti-like tangle of roads going out in all directions, but he knew exactly where to go. There were no road signs but, somehow, he knew. I was glad I was not driving, and really glad I was not biking.

The conversations between the driver and guide were in Kazakh, so it seemed we were really just along for the ride. Ainep would occasionally point out something along the way, explaining about the mountains and terrain. They agreed to stop for photo opportunities, like a small herd of camels grazing just off the road and walking through a light layer of snow on the ground. As we ran out of flat land, the snow-covered mountains appeared closer and larger. In my mind, I could picture a ski resort, with a chairlift to the top and long, unobstructed runs to the bottom over virgin powder snow.

Approaching the Altai Mountains

Darkening skies with increasing snow

Late that morning, Ainep asked if we were hungry and made a phone call to place a lunch order. A short time later, we entered a small village with several houses, a mosque, and a gas station. Akbolat stopped for gas, then drove up to a house. A man in a gray jacket and cap waved us into his home. It was a small, comfortable house, with a living room and a generous kitchen where we all sat at a small table. There may have been a bedroom, but I didn't see one. We were warmly greeted by Katderbil and his wife Earkish, along with their daughters Norkiem and Zanip. Young Norkiem looked to be about four years old and was shy around strangers, yet still curious. She would sneak a peek at us from behind a door, then quickly run away if we saw her.

Earkish prepared a huge lunch of noodles, meat, and diced potatoes on the cast-iron dung-burning stove in the corner of the kitchen, along with milk tea and bread. It was both filling and delicious. Milk tea is made by boiling water and milk (cow, goat, sheep, or camel), then adding a handful of finely ground tea. Once it becomes a light tan color, it is taken off the stove to steep. Traditional noodle and meat dishes were found everywhere throughout Mongolia. Meals were usually sparse on vegetables and heavier on meats, mostly beef or mutton. Depending on availability, Mongolian cuisine might include any of the "five snouts": cow/yak, sheep, goat, camel or horse. Ainep explained our lunch was a typical Kazakh meal. According to her, one of the key differences between Kazakh and Mongolian cooking is that in Kazakh kitchens the meat is cooked longer, making it more tender. This seemed true, since some Mongolian meals I had were a bit chewy, while this one was moist and tender.

After lunch, we walked outside and noticed a yak and her calf wandering just a few yards away. There was no grass anywhere in sight, and it appeared they were looking for garbage to eat. The mother had long black hair and a white stripe down the middle of her snout. Her baby had black and white markings but without the long hair of a yak and looked more like the calf of a dairy cow. They seemed friendly, mostly ignoring us, but I was not going to get too close. I felt sure she knew how to use those horns.

We thanked our hosts for lunch, then climbed back in the Russian van for more bumpy roads. This was the Altai Mountain range, which had beautiful scenery high in the hills. We were now in those snowcapped peaks we had previously seen from a distance. As we climbed in altitude, there was a noticeable drop in temperature. We stopped at one mountain pass just above 9,000 feet for a photo opportunity and were hit by a blast of frigid wind as we stepped out of the van. A tall pole had arrows showing the distances to dozens of cities like London, Buenos Aires, Cape Town, and Sydney. I learned we were 10,379 km from Los Angeles but only a mere 4,090 km from Bangkok. The picturesque mountaintop view was worth the cold, but after a few quick pictures it was back to the warmth of the van.

The long drive continued. It was about seven hours over rocky washboard dirt roads, making very slow progress. The "roads" were nothing more than ruts created in the dirt from other vehicles. With minimal traffic, the road eventually became little more than tire tracks, often obscured by snow.

The trusty Russian van

Finally, we arrived at the end of the road and our destination for the night - Tavan Bogd National Park. This nearly 2,500-square-mile area sits in the Altai Mountains, bordering Russia to the northwest and China to the southwest. The Tavan Bogd peaks are the highest mountains in Mongolia, with some rising over 14,000 feet. Within the park are ancient petroglyphs found in cave complexes, now designated a UNESCO World Heritage Site.

We met Yerzat, the park ranger, and his wife, Jazera, at their remote outpost. The ranger station was made of cinderblock, with two rooms and a corrugated metal roof. Yerzat and Jazera immediately invited us inside, where the kitchen was warm and the stove was cooking food for lunch. We had a hot meal of noodles and meat, along with bread and tea, while getting to know our hosts. They told us we were about 20 km from the Russian border.

There was a yurt next to the ranger station, which was our new home for the night. Entering through the small door we saw brightly colored tapestries along the circular walls, with vivid reds, yellows, whites, and greens against a black background. It was all quite comfortable, with the fire already burning in the cast-iron stove in anticipation of our arrival. The fuel for the fire was, of course, dried animal dung, which I am pleased to say burns well without odor. This is a common practice. Every yurt would have piles of dried dung for a good winter supply of heat. Considering temperatures could drop to -20°F to -30°F at times, it made sense to use inexpensive and widely available resources.

I was given a quick lesson on the difference between gers and yurts. They are basically the same round tents, usually white, with a central stove and beds around the periphery. The word "ger" is Mongolian, but "yurt" is a Kazakh word with roots in the Russian language. Although many fled Kazakhstan because of Russian domination, some customs and language persisted. According to Ainep, yurts are often larger, and the roof is supported by numerous poles with one end inserted into a central ring and the other end anchored to the walls, often without the central vertical support poles found in gers. Both gers and yurts are nomadic in origin and can be put up or taken down in less than two hours.

Later that evening, we had another dinner prepared by the ranger's wife. While we were eating, Yerzat received a call on his radio and had to rescue another tourist van that had become stuck in the snow. We found out later that the ranger was able to get their van moving again, and they turned back to Ulgii. I thought that was a wise decision, since

I would be terrified to be trapped in a van with temperatures below freezing and weather continuing to deteriorate. The cold wind started to blow harder, but the circular yurt remained warm with the central stove producing more heat than I expected. Ainep, Akbolat, Jon, and I each had our own bed along the outer wall, while the fifth bed served as seating and a place to store backpacks.

With no cell towers, Wi-Fi, or any other way to contact home, it seemed sleep was our best option. We each made the short twenty-yard trek to the outhouse before settling in for the night. Most outhouses only had one stall, but this one had four - two on each side. It was still a basic five-plank floor with the middle board missing, but, in an odd way, having four stalls made it feel a bit special. Our little yurt was small but cozy enough for the four of us. We were only going to be there for one night and then leave the next morning, though given the weather, I had doubts about that.

SEPTEMBER 26: SNOWBOUND – TAVAN BOGD NATIONAL PARK

It was a cold night, with brutal, sub-freezing temperatures. I was warm enough wearing several layers of clothing and wool socks inside my down sleeping bag. Inside our yurt, it was above freezing thanks to the dung-fueled stove. Akbolat had to go outside to the dung pile during the night to collect more dung to add to the stove. Dung burns well but does not last very long. I learned that, given the choice, urine-soaked yak dung is preferred. The urine makes it burn slower yet still gives off good heat. This was lifesaving information I never considered needing. Outside our yurt, it was significantly colder, perhaps down to -12°C (10°F) or less. Several times throughout the night I heard the wind increase enough to cause the outside layers of our yurt to flap violently, shaking the entire structure. All I could do was trust that centuries of engineering skill in yurt construction would keep our simple round structure intact for the night.

When we awoke, the stove had gone out, so it was extremely cold when everyone had a need to use the outhouse. Akbolat was the first one up and dressed but had trouble getting the door open. I could see him pushing, but the door wouldn't budge. Jon joined in, and together they pushed it open just enough to see snow covering nearly the entire door. A snow drift had piled against the door, the only door, so it would not open. Inside the yurt, I could see a ring of snow around the door frame where the cold air entered through small gaps during the night. I began to wonder how nomads would handle the situation, since this had surely happened before. After all these centuries with the same design, why hadn't someone thought of adding a second door? Wouldn't that be easier than waiting for the snow to melt? Akbolat and Jon continued pushing hard against the door until they had just enough room to get a hand outside and dig the snow away. It took about thirty minutes or more for the repeated combination of pushing the door and digging the snow to slowly open the door enough to squeeze outside. A full bladder was a great motivator.

After those needs were met at our four-stall outhouse, the remaining snow was cleared, giving us a fully functional door. The dung pile was not far away, and Akbolat had the chore of digging through the snow to find enough dung to fire up the stove. It did not take long before we were warm again. Ainep's chore was to start breakfast. The promised "hearty" breakfast was limited to tea, cookies, and whatever leftovers she could find.

Ranger Yerzat had access to weather information unavailable to us. He told us it would be getting colder with more snow over the next few days. Despite its beauty, the Altai Mountains can be a dangerous place for weather. Cold fronts could come from either China to our south, or Siberia to the north. Being sandwiched between those two regions at this high altitude could make for very harsh conditions. There was a brief discussion of leaving this afternoon and going back to Ulgii. The hike to the glacier was obviously not going to happen, and the events planned for the next few days didn't look likely either. Ainep and Akbolat spoke in Kazakh, and I assumed they were discussing the weather, but I couldn't tell for sure. All I knew was they looked serious and weren't smiling. I began to wonder if the situation was worse than they were telling us. We all wanted to leave, and the final decision rested with them.

Although the early-morning snow had stopped, Ranger Yerzat said the roads were now impassable. It looked like the decision to leave or not had been made for us. They thought we would be stuck for another day, or possibly more. I took in the landscape all around us. The mountains were obscured by low-lying cloud cover, making the usually impressive view underwhelming. Snow was everywhere, and, without trees, there was a barren emptiness as far as the eye could see. The ranger station and the outhouse provided the only distinct contrast to our yurt. The grand four-day adventure in the mountains had become an exercise in boredom, staring at the yurt walls and waiting for the weather to improve. If I only had a bar or two of Wi-Fi...

With an abundance of time on my hands, I had the opportunity to think. I trusted our ranger and tour people, as their safety was also at stake. They knew this area better than I did and may have been in a situation like this before. I felt they would make the best decisions based on the information they had. But, knowing how difficult weather forecasting is - especially in extremely remote areas like this - I began running different scenarios in my mind. Food, shelter, and clothing are essential for survival, and there were limitations on all three. We brought very little food, and the ranger's supply was limited. We were essentially living in a tent under frigid conditions, with animal dung as the only heat source. Of course, the deeper the snow, the more difficult it would be to find and collect dung. Also, my light packing of clothing did not include anything suitable for conditions this extreme. I was still optimistic, but I had to consider the very real possibility of things going badly. I also had no way to inform Val of our situation.

I then noticed a change in Jon. He was quiet, refusing food, and his demeanor had changed. As the morning went on, Jon began complaining of abdominal pain. My first thought was that he had a bad case of gastroenteritis (traveler's diarrhea) likely from tainted food or water. I realized I needed to keep an eye on him and suggested he drink frequent, small amounts of fluids.

By midday, Jon's symptoms became worse. He looked pale and began to throw up, followed by a significant increase in abdominal pain. I became concerned that this could be more than just basic gastroenteritis. The sudden increase in intensity made me wonder if he was developing acute appendicitis, although without proper lab work and imaging studies, I had no way to know about gall bladder issues, kidney stones, or the myriads of other possibilities that cause vomiting, diarrhea, and abdominal pain. Appendicitis, however, was my worst fear. I remembered being taught in medical school that appendicitis was "the great imposter." Symptoms can be vague, or not what is expected in the usual obvious way. We always had to have a high index of suspicion. The retired doctor inside of me began to stress! Stranded in the mountains was no place for a surgical emergency. An untreated ruptured appendix could be deadly, and we had no way of getting out of there. We would need a medical helicopter to evacuate him, but how would we get one, and could they even fly in this weather? The nearest hospital was probably in Ulgii, a considerable distance even by flying. This situation had the potential to develop into a huge disaster.

I checked him out and, gratefully, he did not have a fever. The abdominal exam was nonspecific. There were no clear signs of appendicitis at that time. By early afternoon, his symptoms changed again. I was still worried about early appendicitis, but the development of diarrhea led me to think again about gastroenteritis. That could also be a serious problem, but it was not an emergency yet. I had medications in my first aid bag that would help, but that was back in Ulgii. The tour company was supposed to carry a first aid kit. I believed them. Big mistake! The only medication Akbolat had was activated charcoal, which was used to treat poisonings and overdoses. The classic example would be a toddler who swallowed a grandparent's medication. Giving Jon charcoal might help a little, but the worst thing about charcoal use (as I learned from my time in the pediatric emergency department) is the mess it makes when the kids throw it all up. Since his current condition could be treated symptomatically, I thought we could rely on fluid management. We had bottled water, and I could filter more if needed. I also had packets of electrolytes we added to the water. Considering that was all we could do, it seemed like a reasonable approach – at least as long as things didn't get worse...

Ainep was our guide, and also our cook. She had previously worked with a Mongolian organization to build greenhouses and plant vegetables. She also had experience with food safety and quality programs. With her knowledge of food safety, I was confident that the water she obtained from a nearby stream was boiled appropriately and the food was cooked correctly. Other than the soup and milk tea which had been boiled well, I still filtered everything else I drank. A good water filter removes the bacteria and viruses that can create problems like this. I assumed somewhere in the last few days, Jon had ingested food or water with disease-causing microorganisms.

The ranger came back to our yurt in the afternoon to check on us. I think his main objective, however, was to dig through a certain cabinet to find a bottle of vodka. I wondered if he had been hiding it from his wife! He offered me a taste, but I declined. Jon wasn't feeling well and was still sleeping, so Yerzat returned with the vodka to his station house about twenty yards away. I noticed that Ainep and Akbolat had also disappeared, and I suspected they were all drinking vodka at the ranger station. We were welcome to join them, but I had no interest in that while watching over Jon.

When Ainep and Akbolat returned, they told us the tourist van that was stuck yesterday had tried to make it back to Ulgii but got lost in the snow. They were not sure where the van was or what kind of conditions they were in. The only ranger for this entire region was with us, and I heard no talk of a rescue plan for them. We did hear of another incident involving a Jeep running off the road. Those people were OK, but their Jeep suffered damage. Traveling in those conditions was clearly dangerous, and we realized that we were not getting out of there anytime soon. As long as we had a good supply of dung for the fire and could stay warm, I was OK - at least for now.

My larger concern was about the next few days. I was very worried about Jon's health. What could be done if he became worse? Our limited food and water would run out at some point, and the dung pile couldn't last forever. There were high mountains between us and Ulgii, with unmarked dirt roads buried under snow. The only comfort was knowing that Akbolat, Ainep, the ranger, and his wife all wanted to get out of there too. They knew this terrain well, and I hoped they would devise a plan.

As the evening approached and hunger began to develop, the ranger's wife, Jazera, entered our yurt with a dinner she had just prepared. She made bowls of noodles, meat, and diced potatoes for the three of us who could eat. For Jon, the smell of food - and even just the thought of eating - only added to his nausea.

The fact that the ranger and his wife shared what little food they had was not lost on me. They had planned to be in their winter home by now, at a much lower elevation with better weather and less snow. They stayed in their remote outpost because, even though the tourist season was over, there were a few tourists - like us, and the lost van - still in the area. A third group was told to stay in Ulgii and not venture out because of the bad weather. I didn't know if the other tourist groups were also from Maral Expeditions (as we were) or from different companies, but it seemed the bad weather had caught many by surprise.

After we had eaten, I saw the ranger and his wife get in their four-wheel drive truck and drive away! My heart sank. The ranger was our source for weather information, and I felt safer with him close by. Having the ranger there, with his radio and expertise of the local terrain, was a comfort. Ainep said they were going to check on their kids, who lived about 10 km away. The ranger and his wife knew where the path should be, but their journey would be risky. We later heard they did arrive safely, but it took several hours just to go 10 km. The roads were hazardous, and with the recent additional snow, they could be even worse tomorrow. Without the ranger and his wife, how would we know when conditions were safe to leave?

Up to this point, I had confidence that we would get out of here safely. Now, without the ranger, I had to wonder how concerned we should be. We still had a supply of dung for heat, but the food was getting low. We had noodles for lunch, which was the only real "meal" of the day. Breakfast was tea and a cookie, while dinner was watery soup. We were all hungry, but the small amount of food available needed to be shared. Only Jon, who was still sick, declined food. He was subsisting on electrolyte water.

My mind wandered to the unpleasant thought of getting stuck in a snow drift somewhere in the Russian van. The last weather forecast we had predicted sun without snow, but forecasts were often unreliable. Daytime high temperatures would still be below freezing. The snow would not be melting anytime soon, but with no new snow expected, I wondered if Ainep and Akbolat might consider trying to leave in the morning. The question would be whether the road through the mountains was open. Even though we were already at a high altitude, we would still need to climb further to reach the pass through the mountains at 9,000 feet - assuming we could find it. Without the ranger's radio, we had no real-time weather updates. Ainep's phone was our only means of communication, which only worked at brief, random times. Jon and I also had no way to communicate with our wives about our predicament. If things went bad, either at the ranger's camp or during our effort to travel impassable roads, no one would have any idea where to even begin looking for us! Further complicating our situation was Jon's health. Unless he made an amazing recovery overnight, he wouldn't be in any condition to take a risk like that.

It was another brutally cold night, but my down sleeping bag came through once again, along with a fleece liner, layers of clothes, and a quilt on top. Akbolat was in a good mood. He staggered in about 10

Trying to stay warm

p.m. and decided that it was a good time to start singing while the rest of us were trying to sleep. I didn't recognize the song - it must have been an old Kazakh favorite. I guessed he had been hitting the vodka again.

I was worried about our predicament and had been trying to text Val for two days. Amazingly enough, I received a response to a text I had sent on WhatsApp earlier in the day! I quickly texted back and was able to give her our location and describe our situation. It was a very limited connection, and we couldn't carry on an actual conversation, but I was happy for any contact I could get. We knew there would be times without communication, but that didn't make it any easier. I could only imagine how scary it was for her to have no idea where we were - lost somewhere in the mountains of rural Mongolia. It was a huge relief to finally get a message through.

SEPTEMBER 27: SNOWBOUND – TAVAN BOGD NATIONAL PARK - AINEP'S BIRTHDAY

I was awakened in the early morning hours by the howling wind. It wasn't as loud as the night before, and the yurt wasn't shaking as much, but it was still unnerving. I wondered if the wind was blowing snow off the road or piling more on it.

Daybreak finally arrived and, since the fire in the stove had gone out, no one was eager to get out of their warm sleeping bags to face the cold. Eventually, nature called, and one by one we all got up. Jon had a rough night, making a few trips to the outhouse in the middle of the night. There is a term called "explosive diarrhea," with the key word being "explosive." This large volume of diarrhea has an urgent need to forcefully come out with little to no warning. It was a terrible situation for Jon, who was already feeling awful, and it became total misery. He had to urgently slog the 20 yards to the outhouse, at night, through the snow, with frigid, howling winds. Although I have Jon's permission to be totally graphic in the description of his illness, let's just say he did not always make it to the outhouse in time.

Jon still looked pale and weak, about the same as the previous day. He said the vomiting had decreased, but diarrhea remained a problem. I checked him out again and, while his general abdominal pain persisted, there were no specific tender spots. That, combined with less vomiting and more diarrhea, made me think it was more likely to be gastroenteritis rather than acute appendicitis. His condition was still a major concern, and I felt helpless because I could not do anything to really help him. A bag of IV fluids would have perked him right up, along with medications I had in my bag back in Ulgii. None of those things were available to us.

As the day progressed, we saw sunshine with continued sub-freezing temperatures. The temperature had not been above freezing for the entire time we had been there. The bitter wind made it feel even colder. Akbolat said that by early afternoon he thought enough snow would have melted for us to see the road. I did not see any way snow would melt in those frigid temperatures, but it was Akbolat's decision whether to leave or not. We were still hoping the ranger might return sometime later in the morning, which would give us fresh tire tracks to follow. There were rumors that two Jeeps were coming our way from Ulgii, which would give us additional tire tracks to follow.

Ainep's phone was our only somewhat reliable means of communication, spotty as it was. She had a Unitel SIM card from a large Mongolian cell network which, depending on weather conditions, would sometimes connect. I was happy about this because Ainep was finally able to talk briefly to her children for her birthday. Besides us singing "Happy Birthday" to her, that was her only birthday gift.

Later in the day, Ainep's phone rang, which she answered in Kazakh. Not knowing if it was her family, the ranger, or something else important, I found myself making a futile effort to overhear every word of a language I didn't understand. When the call ended, she said it was the ranger, who would not be returning. The snow was too deep, and it wasn't safe to travel. There was no way we could leave. If and when the Jeeps got through, we would have some updated information. In the meantime, I hoped we had enough dung to stay warm.

It was an odd thought that the highlight of the day was a trip to the outhouse. The snow had stopped, and the sun occasionally peeked through the clouds. The reward for trudging through the snow was seeing the white mountains against the mostly gray sky. There was no movement anywhere, with no animals in sight. The silence was broken only by my footsteps crunching through the snow underneath. Although I admired the scenery, the freezing cold wind was always present, so it did not take long before returning to the relative warmth of the yurt.

Inside the yurt, boredom quickly set in. I studied yurt construction, observing the simple yet ingenious methods used to build it. The wall expanded into a circle, and 20-foot poles extended from the top of the wall to a central ring, creating the roof. I spent considerable time wondering, given the lack of trees, where they found the wood and poles to construct the frame.

I also thought about the Golden Eagle Festival, now only three days away. Jon planned this entire trip so that we would finish in time to attend it. It would be a huge disappointment, especially for Jon, if we missed it. I began to worry about our plan to fly out of Ulgii back to Ulaanbaatar in six days. Surely, we would make our flight. Right?!

The rest of the day was spent catching up on my napping. Sleeping was the best way to avoid stressing about our situation. I am usually optimistic about things, but we were seriously stuck in these frigid mountains without a viable exit plan. Temperatures were below freezing, Jon was sick, and the food was dwindling. Our best option was to hope for a break in the weather and somehow find a dirt path buried under snow to make the day-long trip back to Ulgii. I was not sure about our chances for success. It felt like I was on Mars with no sign of human life in the vast unknown. Would we ever get home?

Adding to the misery was watching Jon struggle. I was hoping his intake would at least match his fluid losses. He was rehydrating as best as he could by frequently sipping electrolyte solution. At times he appeared to gain strength, which was encouraging. The vomiting was improving, and the diarrhea seemed a little less severe. His abdominal pain was still present, although not quite as intense. Appendicitis often develops with a specific point of tenderness in the right lower abdomen. There was no "point tenderness" on his abdominal exam, which was a good sign. The best thing for Jon was to get him out of this frozen disaster! If there was a possibility of leaving anytime soon, he would have to be able to make the long, jarring ride back.

My appetite was still intact and, being hungry, I thought about the menu described in our itinerary. The "hearty breakfast" of tea and a cookie, "delicious snacks" that did not exist, and "mouthwatering dinner" of watered-down soup did not live up to expectations. The "heartwarming lunch" was the only real food of the day, but four days of noodles had become monotonous. To be fair, I was grateful we at least had something to eat. The food was supposed to be supplied at each different location we were to visit. I would have enjoyed eating with shepherds as their herd grazed, or at the horse ranch after a day of riding stallions. In my current state of hunger, I could only imagine the great food we would have had. But none of that happened. No one expected to be snowbound for four days. We did not have any extra food, so we had to take whatever we could from the ranger station. Being stranded gave us limited options.

A 2:00 p.m. phone update from the ranger revealed the road was still impassable. The daily high temperatures continued to be below freezing, with nighttime lows in the single digits. That day the high temperature was -4°C (24°F) but the next day was expected to warm up to a balmy 1°C (34°F.) In those conditions, it could be a two-day trip back to Ulgii. The ranger would not be returning, and the Jeeps never arrived, so there were no tire tracks to follow.

Snowbound

The late afternoon slowly crept along, and the cloud cover began to clear. The night sky revealed a beautiful moon rising over the snowy mountains, set against a dark blue sky filled with stars. With no snow expected and temperatures forecasted to rise above freezing, we hoped to leave in the morning. This could be our chance! I felt like Gilligan, stranded on an uncharted island.

SEPTEMBER 28: TAVAN BOGD NATIONAL PARK TO ULGII

I woke up this day to find the weather sunny - still below freezing but with clear skies. Akbolat and Ainep discussed the conditions and decided it was time to leave. They received no argument from us. We were all tired of being cold, hungry, and living in a yurt for the past four days. This was our best opportunity. It was also a lucky break, considering we were just about out of food. Ainep had already taken everything that could be eaten out of the ranger station.

Another very important break was that Jon had started to feel better. His vomiting, diarrhea and abdominal pain were improving. He looked stronger and had the beginnings of an appetite again. Traveler's diarrhea/gastroenteritis is no fun, but far better than appendicitis and many other causes of abdominal pain. It usually resolves in a few days with fluids and supportive care, and he was following that course. Although Jon was not yet fully recovered, he recognized the opportunity to leave was finally here. He was well aware of the bumps and jarring conditions he would endure on the van ride back and felt up to the task.

At around 9:00 a.m. we loaded up the trusty Russian van and headed down the "road." Given that the road was nearly non-existent, we had a challenge finding our way. From the back seat I was watching Ainep and Akbolat carefully scanning for any bump in the snow that might indicate a buried tire track. Several times we would hit a small snowdrift and get stuck. There was one shovel in the van, so Jon and I took turns digging ourselves out. The snow was knee high in some places, so the main goal was clearing the tires of the four-wheel drive to get traction. Hitting rocks with the shovel meant we were in the dirt, giving us the best traction. After shoveling came the pushing. Jon and I would push while Akbolat gunned the engine and spun the wheels.

After an hour or so, we passed an abandoned yurt camp and saw fresh tire tracks leaving the site. That was lucky, because if they found their way out, then we could follow their trail. Ainep was also able to get a phone call out to the ranger. She let him know our progress and got updated weather information. She told us the ranger wanted to meet with us again, farther down the road at his "summer" house. He and his wife had not yet moved down the mountain to their "winter" house.

After another thirty minutes we saw a small, white, one-level house on a hill. Halfway up the hill was a four-wheel drive Landcruiser that looked like it could climb no farther. These were the tire tracks we were following, so our trail ended here. The ranger came down the hill on horseback to greet us, through snow that was up to the horse's knees. He told us to hike up the hill to his house so we could "make a plan."

Since I wasn't properly prepared for unexpected snow, I was wearing jeans, hiking boots, and my down jacket. This was not ideal for trudging through two feet of snow in freezing temperatures. There is a saying in camping and backpacking that "cotton kills." When cotton clothing (like my jeans) gets wet, it loses the ability to insulate against the cold. This can lead to hypothermia, especially in conditions like this. Unfortunately, I had no choice. My hiking boots and jeans were caked with snow as we slowly climbed the hill. I was trying to follow the tracks made by the horse and those in front of me. In my mind the hill became a small mountain. We all struggled but we made it. My feet were cold but not wet – yet.

At the ranger's house we met the occupants of the Landcruiser. Christine and Vanessa were both tourists from the US, along with their guide, Quantil, and driver, Mukhar. The lost tourist group had been found! The ranger told them to wait until we arrived, thinking it would be safer if both groups traveled together. The two women were the first US citizens we had met on the entire trip, and it was great to hear American accents again. Christine was from California, but originally from New Jersey, growing up not far from where I did. Vanessa lived in New York. They were longtime friends out for adventure. I think their wish came true.

We had brief introductions, discussing where we were from and what we were doing here. The ranger then pointed to the women's bags and told Jon and I to carry all their gear to the Landcruiser. This was the "plan" the ranger had referred to!? My illusions of a hot snack at the ranger's house quickly evaporated. I did not mind helping our new friends, but we had not eaten yet and I was hungry. The women were able to accommodate the smaller luggage, but the remainder was left for Jon and me. Shouldering the backpack was easy, but hoisting their bags high enough to keep them out of the snow while trudging down the steep hill made the load grow heavier with every step. Finally, everything was loaded into their vehicle, and we climbed back into our Russian van. I tried, in vain, to get the crusty snow off my jeans and boots, knowing it would be wet once it melted. I knew that cold and wet would be a bad combination that I would have to endure. Jon wore a pair of big, waterproof boots he had bought at the black market in Ulgii. I did not realize at the time how smart that purchase was.

Akbolat fired up the van, and we left to find the elusive trail home, with the Landcruiser following close behind. At times we could barely make out a possible road, and at other times it was a complete guess. Akbolat would frequently stop and walk around with a shovel, testing the depth of the snow before proceeding. We finally came across fresh tire tracks which we began to follow, having no way of knowing where they would lead. I sat back and looked at Jon. Over the past several days he was seriously ill and had not eaten much. Now he was carrying baggage, shoveling snow, and helping muscle our van from mounds of snow! I wondered if his drive to get out of our snowy nightmare was fueling his energy or if he was some kind of superhero. Perhaps both!

We became stuck several times, repeatedly dug ourselves out, and slowly made what I thought was progress. Very slow progress. Jon and I alternated shovel duty with each snowbank we hit. I was grateful for the van's four-wheel drive and good tires. At times we came to a fork in the trail with equally fresh tire tracks each way. The two drivers would discuss options and hopefully choose the correct trail. A map of our route would show a lot of backtracking and driving in circles.

By midday, with our Russian van leading the way, we came to a steep hill with soft, wet ground. Akbolat attempted to climb it, but the van slid back sideways and became stuck in the snow. And I mean really stuck, with a significant tilt to the right. It felt like we were not far from turning over. Jon and I jumped out and quickly tried shoveling snow, rock, and mud away from the van. We were unsuccessful. Akbolat then developed a new strategy by shoveling at specific spots then gunning the engine, with Jon and I pushing and rocking the van. The more difficult the task became, the more frustrated Akbolat became. I could see the dogged determination in his face. Without any words, we instinctively knew to step away since he was committed to resolving our dilemma. He eventually assumed the sole responsibility of freeing the van.

Being relieved of our job, we noticed Christine and Vanessa at the back of their Landcruiser, tailgate down, having what appeared to be a small party of hot tea and snack food. They invited us to join them, and we eagerly accepted. Even though it was just a small variety of snacks, it felt like a feast. Christine and Vanessa talked about the good food they had while on their expedition, which gave me a tinge of jealousy. It was a world away from our watered-down soup and stale cookies.

While we were eating, Akbolat was still working to get the van out of the ditch. Firing up the engine one more time, we watched as the tilted van slowly righted itself and progressed up the hill. Ten yards later, the van was once again level on solid ground. With the party over, we climbed back into our respective vehicles and were able to continue on our way.

Over the next few hours, we drove slowly over what we hoped were roads. We would occasionally stop so the two drivers could get out and discuss their options. With mountains all around us, and snow covering everything, I was amazed they had any sense of direction at all. The snow appeared flat, but the ground underneath varied, so we would drive into deep snow drifts then have to dig out, back up, and go in a different direction. Progress was slow and time-consuming as the little Russian van powered on.

Heading in the general direction of the mountain pass but clearly being lost, we spotted a small house in the distance, sitting by itself in a large, flat area that might have land for summertime grazing. As we came closer, the tiny black dots I saw from a distance became recognizable as a small herd of goats. I was impressed by how they could find enough grass to eat by digging through the snow. Gradually, we made our way to the house where we were met by two men whom we assumed to be shepherds. Their house was large enough to have two or three rooms, built from what looked like homemade cinder blocks. The shepherds were outside waiting, having spotted us long before we approached.

Our two drivers met the shepherds and began a conversation with them in Kazakh. From the back seat I watched them closely for any hint of what was going to happen next. There were handshakes, head nodding, and arms pointing in different directions. Our driver was pointing high, apparently talking about the mountain pass. The shepherds shook their heads "no" and pointed low in a different direction. Our driver again pointed high, and the shepherds again pointed away. The discussion went this way for nearly ten minutes. Akbolat then returned to the van, looking frustrated, and spoke to Ainep. She told us the shepherds informed Akbolat that the 9,000-foot mountain pass was completely blocked. There would be no way to make it through. The only way out was to take the road near the Russian border. I asked Ainep how "near" the Russian border it would be. Her answer was "yes."

I took a moment to consider our situation. We were trying to find an unknown road through mounds of snow very close to the border with Russia. What were the chances that we might make a mistake and accidently wander into Russian territory? I did not want to be a part of an international incident and surely did not want my wife and kids to see my face on the news being accused of spying. I had heard about Russian prisons and would prefer to stay out of them!

My thoughts were interrupted by one of the shepherds who offered to lead us to the road. We formed a mini-caravan, led by the shepherd on horseback, followed by the Landcruiser and our van. We drove at a walking pace as the shepherd carefully picked his way through the snow. The van droned on, rarely getting out of first gear. We drove that way for half an hour or more before coming to a stop. There were tire tracks in the snow. The shepherd had guided us to the road! We were pointed in the right direction and we thanked him profusely. He and his horse headed back, and we set off to follow the tire tracks.

It was a huge relief knowing we were on the road that should eventually take us to Ulgii. We were still many miles away, but I was more hopeful now than an hour ago. As we passed mountains on our left, Ainep explained that the other side of those mountains was Russia. It looked like it was only a few miles away. I was still concerned about staying on the Mongolian side of the border. Jon and I thought that without our passports, maybe we could tell the border guards we were Canadian. Everyone loves Canada! Of course, I didn't think that would fool anyone. My real hope was that there would be so much paperwork processing two American intruders that the Russian border guards would simply point us in the right direction and send us back to Mongolia.

Akbolat followed the road, and after an hour we encountered a small group of buildings in an encampment at the base of the mountain. I could see a dozen men wearing fatigues and walking near military-looking vehicles. Akbolat was driving straight toward the camp, and I thought he might stop to ask for directions. There was no flag or any insignia to confirm their nationality. Were they Mongolian or Russian?

Our savior on horseback

At the last moment Akbolat made a dramatic turn away from them. That made me nervous. I assumed this was a Mongolian outpost, but Akbolat must have thought it better not to find out. I was sure they had seen us and was grateful they did not come after us to find out who we were. As we departed, there was a fork in the road leading out of the camp. Choosing the more well-traveled one, it took us behind a hill to the trash dump. We backed up, then chose the other fork.

We drove along beautiful snow-covered mountains and by late afternoon the terrain became a little less steep. We were now on a well-defined road with fresh tire tracks. This meant we were not likely to get stuck in any more snowdrifts. I hoped my cold, wet hiking boots might have a chance to dry out. Thankfully the van had heat, so we were comfortable as long as the van was moving.

We continued throughout the afternoon and into the evening. We still had no food, but no one seemed hungry anyway. All we wanted was to make it back to Ulgii, which was about 100 km away. Under these conditions, that could take at least another 6-8 hours. We stopped at a small "village" along the way, the first one we had seen, which consisted of only a few houses. Akbolat called out to an older man walking by, wearing a dark riding coat. They had a brief conversation, Akbolat gave him some money, and the man returned with a glass jug which he poured into our gas tank. There was no gas station here, so I guess he siphoned gas out of another vehicle for us. It was then that I noticed the van's gas gauge was on empty. Akbolat had filled the gas tank when we stopped for lunch on our way to Tavan Bogd a few days ago, but since then we had traveled many miles, much of it in first gear, driving around in circles. I hated to think we came this far and nearly ran out of gas!

Further down the road we found another village with a small market. We were all very hungry by this time and, with just a few food options, I thought the package of instant kimchi noodle soup was the heartiest one. All I had to do was add hot water, which the woman at the market did for me. Ainep offered to arrange a place to stay for the night in one of the small towns along our route. Akbolat said he was fine either way but was willing to continue to Ulgii. Jon and I quickly agreed that making it to Ulgii tonight would be our preference. Our traveling companions in the Landcruiser decided their day was long enough. They opted to stop for the night, so we wished each other well as we parted ways. Although we only knew Vanessa and Christine for a matter of hours, it felt like a touch of home talking to fellow Americans.

As evening turned into night, a beautiful full moon rose over the mountains, glowing in the clear, dark sky. Without city lights nearby, the night was completely lit by stars. I took pictures but they didn't do it justice. It was a beautiful sight. With my hunger satiated and feeling more confident we would make it back to Ulgii that night, I felt my spirits lifting. Jon and I had completed our bike trip across Mongolia, made it out of our snowbound mess, and were still on schedule for the Eagle Festival and flights home. I was happy to look out the van windows and admire the surroundings.

Unfortunately for Akbolat, he had no time for sightseeing while remaining totally focused on driving in the darkness. It was difficult enough to find a snow-covered dirt road in daylight, but now in the dark with windblown snow, it was even more difficult. There were no other vehicles with lights or new tire tracks to guide us. We had to proceed slowly to avoid rocks, ruts, and the occasional goat that thought the middle of the road would be a good place to stand. Further on we passed a few horses and some cows not far from the road, just standing out in the cold. I knew they were accustomed to being outside all night in sub-freezing temperatures, but I sure felt sorry for them.

It was around 11 p.m. when, in the distance, I saw the faint lights of a city – Ulgii. I was confident Akbolat would get us back and, after four days in a cold yurt, the city was a wonderful sight. It seemed like an enormous amount of time until we passed the airport, where in a few days we would be flying out. We finally drove down streets that looked familiar. Ainep had phoned ahead to Bota and arranged for a pizza to be waiting for us on arrival. It was good to be in our Mongolian "home" again.

Arriving just after midnight, the 15-hour drive home from our snowbound adventure was finally over! The return trip had taken over twice as long as the one from Ulgii to Tavan Bogd National Park. That was just a few days earlier but seemed like ages ago. I gave our driver, Akbolat, a huge amount of credit for finding our way out of the mountains. I considered him a hero because without him, I'm not sure how we would have made it safely back to civilization. I had been comfortable with biking during this trip, and quite confident I could handle the physical challenge. The past four days, however, made me feel vulnerable, dealing with conditions well out of my control. Among the many stressors we encountered, Jon's health situation was the most disturbing. If it had become worse, there was nothing I could have done to help him. I didn't want to think about the conversation I would have been forced to have with Jon's wife if something bad happened to him. It was a frightening, helpless feeling I hope to never experience again.

SEPTEMBER 29: ULGII

The day was not as exciting as the previous one, which was alright with me. I was just happy to be back in Ulgii. I felt safe again, confident that we had successfully endured through the most dangerous part of the trip. Nothing was expected over the next few days that would interfere with the Eagle Festival or our flights home. By this time next week, I would be home!

There were only two goals that day – finish my Christmas shopping and see if there was a way to ship the bike to my son in North Carolina. He was looking for a mountain bike and, while this one was a little beat up, I had been happy with it. My bike and I spent a lot of time together, and I had grown attached to it. The Alton Sandstone Mountain bike was new when purchased in Ulaanbaatar. We added upgrades like a more comfortable seat, hybrid tires, and a few extra features. It was still a solid bike, despite the wear and tear, which should meet his needs. Besides, there was a "cool" factor being the Mongolian bike.

The problem was how to ship it. I needed a box, and I knew the best place to find a box for a bicycle was a bike store. Google maps did not identify a bike store in town, so I did the next best thing - I asked a kid with a bike. He told me there was a bike store about one kilometer away, near the bridge, as he pointed in the direction. Google maps showed where the bridge was, so I headed that way.

I found the bike store, but it was closed. I assumed that since it was Friday, it would be a normal business day. The large glass windows showed several bikes inside, but no one was there. The sign on the door had a phone number, so I called and asked if they spoke English. I think I heard a "no" mixed in with a lot of Mongolian before they hung up.

The next plan was to call Ainep for help. She checked a few places and found someone who had a box for a bicycle at his home. Ainep said Akbolat agreed to pick it up and deliver it to me. That was a lucky break. So, if I had a box, and I knew where the post office was, all I needed was packing tape. I wandered around the shops outside the town square, hoping to find one that sold packing tape. Most of the shops were small, and I could not read the signs printed in Mongolian. Nothing looked like a hardware store, and I began to get frustrated.

In an amazing coincidence, a man on the sidewalk coming toward me was carrying two rolls of packing tape in his hand. I thought this had to be ovoo karma! I stopped him, pointed to his tape, and motioned that I needed some. He pointed down the street and said "tock," which I interpreted was the name of the store where he bought it. Now all I had to do was find the "tock" store, which did not translate well. I saw a supermarket that looked promising, and in the small hardware section I found five-roll packs of packing tape, one with two rolls missing. This had to be where the man on the street found his two rolls of tape!

With everything I needed, what could go wrong? Well, the box arrived, and it was for a child's bike. There was no way I could pack my bike to fit in that small box. I would need a second box for the wheels, and I didn't have the time or resources to find one. The chances of my son getting the bike were now pretty slim. At least I had time to finish the rest of my Christmas shopping. Maybe my son would be happy with a nice pair of Mongolian slippers instead!

SEPTEMBER 30: THE GOLDEN EAGLE FESTIVAL – DAY ONE

This was the day Jon had been looking forward to for a very long time. Everything about this trip was planned so that we could attend this festival. Jon works closely with native tribes in Alaska and has great respect and admiration for cultural heritages. He explained to me what he knew about the Eagle Festival, which piqued my interest and curiosity. I was looking forward to an amazing experience.

The Golden Eagle Festival is an annual event and the largest of its kind, attracting people from all over the world. Its traditions date back centuries, even before the time of Chinggis Khaan. Eagle hunters acquire eggs from nests and train their eagles beginning as chicks. The eagle imprints with the hunter to become a devoted teammate. The eagles are trained to hunt small animals and return them to their humans. Many of today's contestants can trace the family heritage of eagle hunting back several generations. It is a male-dominated activity, but over the past several years women have competed as eagle hunters too. There is an excellent film from 2016, *"The Eagle Huntress,"* that Val and I watched on YouTube before the trip began. It is the story of a 13-year-old Kazakh girl who was the first female to compete in the Golden Eagle Festival in Ulgii. Spoiler alert: she wins the competition as the men stood back in amazement. Doing well in an eagle hunting competition, especially at this high level, is extremely difficult and a tremendous honor.

Ainep and Akbolat arrived early in the morning, right on schedule, to take us the 15 km to Shar Lake, the site of the festival. The parking lot was already busy when we arrived, with lines of identical gray Russian vans from various tour companies all parked together. Hundreds of spectators were already there, and by the end of the day there would be a thousand more.

There were plenty of men in impressive traditional Kazakh dress with hooded eagles on their arms, posing for pictures. The hoods are used to block the eagle's vision, which calms them. If the eagle can't see a threat, then there is no threat. The eagle hunters had the look of fierce warriors holding their majestic birds, while allowing large crowds of curious onlookers to admire them up close. Some of the men wore brightly embroidered clothing with intricate designs, while others wore fur and leather.

Eagles are revered and loved as family

There was a large area of yurts, with food and merchandise for sale. It reminded me of tailgating before a college football game. Smoke and the smell of food cooking was in the air. Several yurts were mini-restaurants, serving bread and noodles with mutton or other meats. A large central area had brightly embroidered tapestries for sale, laid out on the snow-covered ground. Those in need of fur hats or cold weather clothing were also in luck. I took a step back to watch the crowd, half of

The real thing

whom wore Western or European clothing while others wore Kazakh or Mongolian. It was a harmonious blend of cultures, with down jackets standing next to embroidery and fur.

Along the perimeter were several other yurts featuring exhibits. One featured local archeology, with photos of ancient petroglyphs carved in rock, found in caves within the Altai Mountains. The various rock carvings depicted rams, animals with antlers, and a hunter with bow and arrow. Another yurt had an exhibit of traditional Kazakh embroidery. Two women were busy inside hand-stitching the complex designs. Their experienced fingers moved quickly and effortlessly. It was an impressive, time-honored skill. Still another row of yurts held exhibitions on artwork, cultural heritage, wildlife science, and conservation, among other things. This area alone was worth the trip, but there was still more to see!

I made my way to an area somewhat hidden behind a large hill and saw a crowd circling the main arena. The football-field-sized oval arena was fenced off, with large crowds standing on the near side and a booth on the far side for the announcer and judges. A string octet was seated in front of the announcer's booth, playing traditional Kazakh music. Along with violins and cellos, there were other stringed instruments I was less familiar with - probably dombras, which are small instruments with a long neck and two strings. The music was unfamiliar, and I couldn't identify a type of genre. It had a very pleasant classical sound with an Asian flair, with almost a "pop" kind of feel to it. I wondered how this music could be performed back home, maybe as featured artists with a local symphony. I thought it might be a big hit. I would enjoy it!

When the previous music ended, another group of musicians, dancers, and singers emerged. As the music played, male and female dancers moved to the rhythm, with the women spinning their long dresses with every turn. The Kazakh folk dance reminded me of the traditional Mexican dances I had seen at large Cinco de Mayo festivals.

The last performer was a man who played a solo dombra piece. I didn't catch his name but, apparently, he was quite a famous musician in this area. He produced an amazing number of beautiful melodies with only two strings.

After the music concluded, the "Eagle Hunter's Parade" began. All the participants rode single file on horseback into the arena, with hooded eagles perched on their right arms. The riders, dressed in fur and riding clothes with Kazakh embroidery, looked both fierce and regal at the same time. I wondered if this was what the Mongol army looked like in the days of Chinggis Khaan. The horses made a soft pounding sound, kicking up snow as they passed by. I could not tell if the announcements were in Kazakh or Mongolian, as they sounded similar and were both unintelligible to me. Occasionally we would hear an announcement in English, which was very helpful. The announcer explained that over 140 eagle hunters had signed up for the day's event. By the end of the day that number increased to 156 participants - the largest event ever held.

The first competition was "Calling the Eagle," which involved a handler bringing the hooded eagle to the top of a large hill. The eagle's owner, the eagle hunter, rode a horse in the arena below. When the eagle hunter was ready, he signaled the handler by waving his arms and yelling. The handler removed the hood while the rider called out with a series of loud yells. The eagle is supposed to recognize his master's call and fly down about 100 yards to perch on the eagle hunter's arm, with the fastest time winning. It was a spectacular sight, watching these beautiful birds gracefully fly down with wings extended and perching as expected. Many landed within thirty seconds. One competitor, a 13-year-old girl, had her eagle land in 24 seconds. She was one of the top finishers.

Not all the eagles cooperated. Once the hood came off, some of the eagles just wanted to fly around in circles and enjoy a brief taste of freedom. Those who failed to perch did not fly very far away. When their owner rode over to them, the eagle obediently flew up to perch on their extended arm. One wayward eagle landed on, or perhaps tried to attack, a child standing on the hillside. The eagle hunter and his horse took off like a lightning bolt toward the child and quickly brought the eagle under control. There was a bit of commotion as a small crowd gathered to help. After a few minutes, everyone was able to walk away with the child seemingly unharmed. As a newcomer to eagle hunting, I realized this sport was much more dangerous than I thought.

As we continued to watch the eagles' flight paths, wondering if they would perch on the arms of their eagle hunters, I was hit in the back of the head by a snowball. I turned around and saw an angelic looking ten-year-old girl with her eight-year-old brother, both wearing an innocent "what happened?" expression. I turned back to watch the eagles and was hit by another snowball. Jon also got hit, and that meant we were free to fire back. I lobbed a few snowballs in their direction, not intending to hit them, but that angelic girl had a rifle for an arm. She was 15 yards away and deadly accurate. I thought it was too bad they did not have a baseball team - she would have made an excellent pitcher. Her brother also had an amazing arm for an eight-year-old.

Since we were on the losing end of this exchange, and not wanting it to get out of hand, I called a truce and went over to shake hands and congratulate them on a good snowball fight. As I turned and walked back to Jon, another snowball beaned me in the back of my head. I was tempted to fire back, but I thought it was best to admit defeat and go back to being a spectator.

After the snowball fight, we were free to roam around and meet the eagle hunters. Those who were not competing were happy to pose for pictures and talk with tourists if a common language existed. If not, money seemed to help. It was absolutely worth a few dollars of tugriks just to be near these hunters and their prized birds. I was touched to see the eagles treated with such love and respect by the hunters.

In between eagle flights, I noticed a camel sitting contentedly on the ground. Bactrian camels are native to Mongolia and the steppes of Central Asia. Several people were petting him and taking photos, so I joined in too. I had only seen camels in zoos and had never been close enough to touch one. The hair was thick and coarse, which I suppose provides insulation for the harsh conditions they endure. The camel not only tolerated the tourists, but I think may have enjoyed the attention.

After meeting my first camel, I easily found Jon in the crowd – the tall man wearing a Green Bay Packers cap. With so many competitors, the eagle calling competition consumed the entire day. We were told the activities scheduled for the next day would move faster. We had already seen a lot and were excited about the next events. There was much to fit into a two-day festival. As our first day ended, we loaded into the Russian van and drove back to our cold little house.

OCTOBER 1: THE GOLDEN EAGLE FESTIVAL – DAY TWO

The eagle festival was a unique experience, and we were curious and excited to see more. The competitions seemed a bit bizarre to me, although I appreciated and respected the cultural heritage they represented. Day two began with "Attacking a Chargai," where the eagle hunter trots into the arena dragging a fox or rabbit fur lure behind his horse to test his eagle's speed and precision. The eagle is released from the hillside and flies down to attack the fur lure. This was another timed event, with the fastest time winning. Most of the eagles flew in a circle or two before swooping down on the fur. A few of them knew their jobs well, immediately focusing on their prey and making a direct line of attack. We were told by one of the many tour guides that an eagle attacked someone's dog the day before. Apparently, the dog suffered only minor injuries. That eagle was then considered a great hunter, becoming very valuable to its owner who would be offered a large sum of money if he decided to sell it.

The next event, the "Kukbar," was an intense competition to demonstrate horsemanship skills. The event involved two riders pulling on a decapitated goat carcass with both hands, while maneuvering the horse through tight turns at a full gallop. The riders, barely holding on with only their knees and legs, continued the tug-of-war until one of

Preparing for the day's events

the riders was either forced to let go, or was dragged off their horse. This was a centuries-old Mongolian tradition, dating as far back as the time of Chinggis Khaan. They still use a goat carcass to this day, staying true to the old ways.

The "Kukbar" demonstrates horsemanship skills using a goat carcass

Later in the day we witnessed an event I thought was unusual called the "Kiz-Kuar." This contest highlighted the riding skills of both women and men, each riding on opposing horses in the arena. The woman, with her whip swinging, chased the man around the arena as the man tried to ride fast enough not to get caught. I was told she had the option of beating him with her whip if she caught him, but fortunately it usually ended in a kiss. The couple with the fastest time around the arena won. Most of the women in the crowd seemed to like that event.

While the events in the arena were going on, I noticed a disturbance outside the arena. There were several riders with whips chasing a single man trying to escape at a full gallop. The riders caught him, and the whips went flying. It wasn't long before the police arrived and tried to restrain the mob, which made the scene even more chaotic. A police van drove up, and the man being beaten was put inside and taken away. There were guides nearby from different tour companies who spoke English, and I asked them what was happening. One guide explained that it was "mountain justice" being served. Rumors circulated that the man was caught stealing or had a grudge against the judging. Either way, the man was probably happy the police were there to take him away in the police van. I am sure Mongolian jails are not pleasant, but perhaps better than getting whipped by an angry mob.

One of the highlights of the day for me was the opportunity to sit on a horse with an eagle on my arm. There was no set fee, but 10,000-20,000 tugriks ($3-6 USD) seemed like the going rate. To me, six dollars was a shockingly reasonable price to pay for this huge, once-in-a-lifetime opportunity. When would I ever get this chance again?

The eagle hunter wore a red, fur-lined hat and a heavy coat of tan and white pelts. Beneath the fur, he wore an embroidered blue shirt that looked like silk, tan leather pants, and black boots. He gave me the reins to his handsome horse, mostly white with black legs, and I mounted the saddle. On the eagle hunter's right arm, the hooded eagle was perched on a thick leather glove that ran the length of his forearm. He took off the glove, with the eagle still perched, and pulled it onto my right arm. I appreciated how thick the glove was as I viewed the eagle's sharp talons. I estimated the bird weighed about 15 pounds, with another pound or two for the glove. The eagle had mostly brown feathers, with white flecks

At the Golden Eagle Festival

in the tail. I had a very close view of the sharp, curved beak. I could see how useful it was for hunting prey. Lucky for me, a bird wearing a hood is not likely to be aggressive but, just to be sure, I tried not to startle it. I quickly realized that if I gently rotated my forearm back and forth, the eagle felt unsteady and instinctively spread out its wings. A woman in the crowd offered to take my phone for pictures. She was very trigger happy and took many photos from different angles, coming up with some amazing shots.

I would have been content if my day had ended there, but another interesting opportunity caught my eye. Just behind the crowd of people surrounding the main arena, a female tourist was sitting on a camel. Since I had never sat on a camel before, I was intrigued. As I approached, the woman dismounted the camel and began a spirited conversation with the camel's owner, along with a policeman who had been called over.

When their lengthy conversation ended, I asked the woman about what had happened, hoping I could still get a camel ride. With a British accent, she introduced herself as Patricia. The camel did not have a name so, in my head, I named him Mark Camel. (Any Star Wars fans reading?) Patricia told me she had paid 10,000 MNT ($3 USD) for a ride and thought that was a fair price. She went on to express concern that the camel's humps were sagging, which was an indication of poor health. It turned out that Patricia knew a lot about camels. She later told me about her time in Morocco, working with and buying camels for a non-governmental organization. Patricia explained that camel humps are primarily used for fat storage, and the humps will sag in malnourished or dehydrated camels. Her discussion with the police officer had been about pressuring the owner to get the camel to water. Patricia was insistent that the owner walk Mark to a lake about a mile away. The camel's owner was reluctant to do so because walking the camel to the lake and back would take precious time away from tourists and potentially cause a loss of income. The solution was to have a tourist (me) pay to ride the camel to the lake. When I offered 20,000 MNT for the ride, the owner was more than happy to oblige.

The owner, wearing a black riding coat trimmed with green embroidery, had the camel kneel to allow me to get on his back. I sat between the humps on a large red blanket with yellow and gold embroidery which had two holes for the humps to protrude. I felt a slight jostle as the camel got to his feet, and I held tightly to his coarse hair to maintain my balance. Once up, sitting between the two wobbly humps formed a natural saddle. I felt like Lawrence of Arabia, walking across the desert. I enjoyed the gentle rocking motion with every step taken by Mark Camel, led by the owner, with Patricia walking beside us.

We did not even get halfway to the lake before the owner abruptly stopped and motioned "no more." He tried to turn the camel around but was stopped by Patricia, who was adamant about getting to the lake. They began a heated discussion in two different languages, where neither understood the other's words, but the meanings were clear. The owner prevailed, but hopefully a small victory was won with my 20,000 MNT helping support his family, and the camel too. I felt sure that living in their harsh mountain climate was difficult for both people and animals. I hoped my small contribution would help.

OCTOBER 2: ULGII

The last day in Ulgii was a pleasant one. Jon had boxes to ship back home but otherwise we both had all our sightseeing and shopping goals accomplished. I wanted to send the bike to my son, but I had no way to do it. Instead, I gave it to Akbolat as a tip. I was grateful he had brought us home safely from our snowbound adventure and thought he deserved it. Since he did not speak English, I had to gesture several times so that he understood I was giving the bike to him. He was surprised and seemed delighted to receive it. The bike was important to me, as it enabled me to travel the Mongolian countryside like Chinggis Khaan on his trusty steed. I doubted Akbolat would feel that way, but I was sure he would enjoy riding it.

I had one final day to wander around Ulgii, a town I had come to know fairly well. I walked down the dirt road from our house to the busy main street. The snow on the ground had mostly disappeared, but it was still cold, with that Colorado feeling of snowcapped mountains visible just beyond the edge of town. The familiar street had apartment buildings and a supermarket. I walked by several nondescript buildings with signs I couldn't read. I passed several locals on the sidewalk, all going about their normal daily routines.

Ulgii was large enough to have plenty of people and stores to provide for one's needs, yet small enough not to have the crazy big-city traffic of Ulaanbaatar. Jon and I enjoyed the restaurants and coffee shops, and the locals we met were all so friendly. I found myself more relaxed in Ulgii, partly because we had successfully completed the trip, but also because the town itself had a certain charm. I had mixed feelings about this being our last day. I felt a strong sense of accomplishment by completing this epic adventure, along with a degree of personal growth from having a better understanding of both the people and the ways of Mongolia. I probably would have enjoyed exploring the area more, but the flight leaving the next day was the first step to going home. As much as I liked Ulgii, home was more important!

As I was walking, the sound of music caught my attention. An eight-piece brass band was warming up in a courtyard between buildings. I could not tell whether their uniforms were police, fire department, or military. They played jubilant songs and, although I did not recognize any of them, the music seemed perfect. The band only played a few pieces before loading up in their Russian van and leaving for their performance, but I would have enjoyed hearing more. I took a shortcut across the town square back to the black market. It was the final chance to get another unique Christmas gift. No matter what day it was, the black market was always a busy place.

Goyo texted me from her office in Ulaanbaatar asking me to return her Mobicom SIM card. She loaned it to me at the beginning of the trip in case my Verizon card was out of cell tower range, and it came in handy several times. She said she had a tour group in Ulgii for the Eagle Festival who would be with us on our 9:40 a.m. flight to Ulaanbaatar the next morning. Her driver would be meeting the group in Ulaanbaatar, and I could give him the SIM card on arrival at the airport. I agreed but explained that our flight departed Ulgii at 2:15 p.m. Olly made the reservation for us weeks earlier because there was only one flight a day from Ulgii to Ulaanbaatar and he wanted to make sure we were on it. I had a copy of the printed confirmation. A short while later she texted again, stating that AeroMongolia had changed our flight. Since Olly booked the ticket through Goyo Travel, they were notified, and we were not. With the once-daily flight to Ulaanbaatar sold out for the next several days by Eagle Festival tourists, this chance text from Goyo potentially saved us from being stuck in Mongolia for who knows how long! We averted the embarrassment of showing up for a flight in the afternoon that had already left that morning!

I spent the afternoon packing and drinking the last bottle of our Tiger beer, a pretty good Mongolian brew. I started out thinking I had plenty of room for everything and finished wondering how I made it all fit. I thought I might need to wear a few layers of clothes home. The winter jacket I had brought was a nice, warm jacket, but I could do without it. I thought the folks in Mongolia might need it more. Ainep was the lucky recipient, and I hoped it would fit either her husband or son. I freed up extra room in the backpack without the jacket and biking gear, but that space quickly filled with Christmas presents.

This trip had been an amazing adventure, but I was more than ready to go home. Val and I would be celebrating our 30th wedding anniversary soon, and this was by far the longest we had ever been apart. Even though I tried calling her every chance I could, depending on Wi-Fi and cell towers, it was just not enough. It did not matter if we discussed routine things, like the kids or college football; it was just hearing her voice that was important. I was grateful that most phone conversations were as clear as a normal call would be at home. But even that was no substitute for being with her. Many times, a text would get through when a voice call would not. It was still comforting to know she was on the other end of the text. It had been a long trip, and I was ready to get home. Adventures are fun, but home was still home.

I was also not embarrassed to say that I missed our dog, Ziggy. Before I left, I tried to explain to him the adventure I was planning. I told him I would be gone for a long time, but I don't think he understood. He just looked at me, probably thinking I was talking about his treats. I hoped he would still remember me when I got home.

The last evening in Ulgii was filled with anticipation. Our AeroMongolia tickets for the 9:40 a.m. flight, as well as our next flight from Ulaanbaatar to Seoul on October 4th, were both confirmed. The last segment, Seoul to home, was less certain. Jon and I both just happen to have sons who are commercial airline pilots, meaning we can benefit from "non-revenue" standby flights if there are open seats available. I had always understood that international flights were rarely full, so non-rev flying should (theoretically) be easy. But when I called my son, he said the 284-seat aircraft had only ten open seats. I began to worry. His airline had only one flight a day out of Seoul, and with the weekend approaching, the passenger loads looked very full. I faced the possibility of being stuck in Seoul for a few days. That would be a tough one to explain to my wife - and the dog, for that matter. So, I did the only reasonable thing and bought a ticket. Sure, it was expensive, but being home on time...priceless!

OCTOBER 3: ULGII TO ULAANBAATAR

The day began early, with Akbolat meeting us at 7:00 a.m. for the ride to the airport. Jon and I were packed and ready to go. The trusty Russian van made its way down the dirt road and turned towards the airport. We did not get far before we encountered a herd of cows and yaks slowly walking along, taking up the entire road. We had to stop the van and wait for them to pass. My first thought was what a large herd it was for being in the city since there was not much land for grazing. Then I realized they were not there to graze - they were going to the slaughter-house! They seemed to know where they were going, with their heads down low and walking ever so slowly. It was a sobering realization. I prefer a primarily vegetarian diet. Val and I rarely eat red meat. However, on this trip, vegetables had been hard to find, and I had eaten my share of noodles and meat. The meat was most likely sheep, cow, or yak. The ugly truth is that the slaughterhouse was a necessary evil. Herders, like farmers, feed the masses. They raise the herd, sell the herd, then do it all over again next year. I understood that meat production was a business. It is nothing personal. Livestock are not given names, and they are not pets. This is a way of life that has been going on all over the world for centuries. I guess, like many modern Americans, I prefer not to think about it. Then again, animals don't march their last parade down my street at home.

The Ulgii airport was just a short drive out of the city. The single airport terminal was small and packed with people when we arrived. MiatMongolian Airlines had a flight leaving just before ours, so two groups of passengers were crammed into the small waiting area, all wanting to check in. The passengers for the earlier flight had priority, so we patiently waited. Jon and I became great friends during this adventure, but seven weeks away from home was a long time. We were both looking forward to our flights home.

After an hour of leaning against a wall in the waiting area, our turn finally came. We slowly advanced in the mass of people toward the check-in counter. We showed the gate agent our tickets and passports, and he instructed us to put our bags on the conveyor belt. The bags moved along and disappeared behind a wall. Next was the metal detector, just a few feet away. It took a surprisingly long time for everyone to go through individually and then wait for the green light to flash, indicating they had cleared the process. After nearly an hour, we finally made it through security. The screening area emptied into a larger waiting room with rows of hard plastic chairs. It was good to finally sit down.

We saw our AeroMongolia plane land, taxi, and park close to the terminal. It was a sleek, modern aircraft painted blue and white, with an emblem of an eagle on the tail. The jet engines in the back reminded me of the CRJ type of aircraft my son flew. The plane arrived empty, with no passengers or baggage. It filled quickly with a packed waiting area full of people heading to Ulaanbaatar. We walked in a line out to the tarmac and climbed up the steps to the door of the plane. It did not take long for us to find our seats and buckle in. The 60-seat jet took off down the only runway, bouncing with every crack in the cement it hit. It was not as jarring as biking over washboard dirt roads, but it was bumpier than I thought a runway should be. We were quickly airborne, gaining altitude flying over the streets of Ulgii and surrounding mountains. The recognizable landmarks disappeared into vast stretches of empty land, with barely a road visible.

The flight to Ulaanbaatar had marvelous scenic views that I was lucky enough to see from my window seat. I wondered what Chinggis Khaan would think about seeing his empire from this view. The wide-open steppe appeared even larger from this altitude. There were occasional threads of roads, and I wondered if they were ones we had biked. What took us weeks to travel by bike is what we were now covering in a three-hour flight. I not only felt a huge sense of accomplishment, having completed this journey of over 1,200 miles, but also the anticipation of soon being home. I just wanted to sit on our deck with my wife, our dog, and a glass of wine.

As our arrival time neared, the city of Ulaanbaatar emerged in the distance. I was again taken by the view of the densely packed urban areas, while outside the city boundary, the vacant land immediately spread out. The landing approach took us past the same windmills I had seen flying into Ulaanbaatar all those weeks ago.

Ulaanbaatar had two airports, the "old" mostly abandoned airport (ULN) and the "new" Chinggis Khaan International Airport (UBN) which opened in 2021. The new airport had one terminal and a single runway, but without the bumps that the Ulgii airport had. It was spacious, clean, and modern, yet small enough to be easy to navigate. Although I was aware of the two airports, I still somehow managed to book our hotel room near the wrong one. I think the free airport shuttle advertised online lured me in. One thing they forgot to mention was the "free" fare was only in one direction. The ride back to the airport cost $20 USD.

After a 25-minute drive toward the "old" airport, we arrived at our hotel in Eagle Town, a suburban district on the edge of Ulaanbaatar. The streets were busy with traffic as we passed by one-story shops between tall apartment buildings. There was a sports arena with a domed roof, reminding me of a smaller version of the Louisiana Superdome in New Orleans. We had booked a two-bedroom suite on the 16th floor overlooking the airport, while also giving us a beautiful view of the city. The outside balcony was a great place to sit if you had a jacket on. It was still a bit cool and windy, but we no longer had to endure the freezing mountain weather. Even though the hotel was terrific, looked new, and had friendly staff, there were only a few rooms booked. I imagine they lost a great deal of business when the airport moved. Within walking distance, we found a huge supermarket with a pizza place inside, conveniently located next to the beer aisle. Someone had planned well.

The evening looked like it would be a low-key night. I hoped to sleep better in the soft bed than I had on the sofa. Tomorrow's breakfast was planned for 8:30 a.m., and the shuttle service back to the other airport was scheduled for 9:30 a.m. We thought this would give us plenty of time to check in for our 1:05 p.m. flight to Seoul. Home was getting closer with each passing minute.

OCTOBER 4: ULAANBAATAR TO SEOUL

After our much-needed rest at the Eagle Town Hotel, the driver took us back to the Chinggis Khaan International Airport. About the size of an airport in any medium-sized city in the US, it was in use for two years and still had a "new" feel to it. With signage in both Mongolian and English, the check-in counter was easy to find, and the screening process went smoothly. It was a huge relief to find the departure gate in plenty of time, and without any problems. Soon enough, we were on the three-hour flight to Seoul.

The Korean Air flight was uneventful, and the flight crew was polite and professional. After the routine flight announcements in Mongolian, Korean, and English were completed, I had time to reflect on the past seven weeks. It began with feelings of curiosity, excitement, and apprehension. I had confidence in Jon's planning and the research I did, but there was no way to really know what we would encounter along the way. What I found was a beautiful yet rugged land, filled with friendly, generous people. Mongolians are proud of their heritage and honor the past by carrying on ancient traditions. We felt welcomed wherever we went, and I was grateful to have visited this mysterious place.

We took a similar flight path to when we first arrived, flying over China and the Yellow Sea on the way to Seoul. From the air, Mongolia and China look similar, mostly brown land between mountains covered in snow. It was difficult to pick out any cities, roads, rail lines, or other man-made features. I thought about the Chinese people who, like the Mongolians, were probably living day to day just trying to get by. I thought about the farmers and shepherds below us not noticing the airplane above them, endlessly working like they do every day.

My stay in Mongolia was short, but I felt less like a tourist and more like a witness to their real way of life. Having the privilege of getting to know the people gave me an ability to respect and truly care about them. I hoped that I had given them that same opportunity. I truly believe that if we could just look at each other with curiosity instead of fear, the world would change for the better.

Our landing approach to Seoul was smooth, with a soft touchdown. The Seoul Incheon International Airport is one of the busiest airports in the world, rivaling the passenger volume of Los Angeles International Airport. The two terminals were nearly identical, both very modern with spotlessly clean tile floors. The restaurants had a wide variety of cuisine, and I especially enjoyed the Asian food while sitting in a quiet area away from the crowds. I had plenty of time to sit, as the one-daily flight to Dallas had departed just before we arrived. This meant that I would be spending the next 24 hours at the airport. I could have left for a hotel, but there were sleeping areas in the airport, and I didn't feel like schlepping my bags throughout the city. My large backpack, small backpack, and gear bag fit on a wheeled luggage cart, which easily maneuvered around the airport. I thought I could get by that way.

The time Jon and I spent together on this final day was relatively short. Jon had contacted his pilot son and was able to arrange an earlier flight to Minneapolis. I was happy for him, and a bit jealous, that he was leaving so soon. He would be home before I even left the airport. With his bags checked and his ticket and passport in hand, we made it to the security screening area. With a hug and well wishes, we said goodbye to each other. Jon then entered the security screening area and disappeared. It felt strange that my good friend, someone I barely knew two months ago, was leaving. Jon and I had been together every day for the past seven weeks. We had been through an incredible adventure, seen some amazing sights, and experienced times of uncertainty. Throughout it all, I could always depend on Jon. He had been envisioning and planning this trip for years, well before I was a part of it. I will always be grateful to him for allowing me to ride his coattails and participate in this epic adventure.

Having lost my traveling companion, I felt a bit lonely. A large void seemed to open. I reassured myself that it was only for one more day. With time on my hands, I roamed around the airport looking for things to do. There were 18-20 long rows of ticket counters, with several different airlines represented on each row. Large queues of passengers waited at each counter to check in. There were airlines from all over the world, with many from the Indo-Pacific regions well represented. Almost half of the airlines were ones that I had never heard of, going to places unfamiliar to me.

I passed the time by going to ticket counters that were not busy and asking for a blank luggage tag. Most just gave me a couple while others asked if I was flying on their airline. When I told them I wasn't, some refused, saying that they cost the airline money. Finally, after collecting a handful of various tags, I got bored and moved on.

I then began to eavesdrop on conversations and enjoyed trying to figure out what languages they were speaking. Rarely did I hear an English voice. Most sounded like they were from an Asian country, but I had a difficult time telling them apart. I thought I could distinguish Mongolian and Korean, but with destinations throughout China, Europe, India, Vietnam, Thailand, the Middle East, and dozens of other locations, I really had no way of knowing.

Watching people was another fun pastime. I saw several young kids who looked excited about going on some big travel adventure, maybe their first time flying, which made me smile. Their happy faces told it all. I was particularly drawn to the clothing people wore, and I noticed most people dressed nicely. The clothing ranged from very casual to very refined. Many wore traditional attire, giving a clue to their country of origin. A few had ornate headwear giving an air of elegance. I saw a few women wearing sarongs that I thought were quite vibrant.

Another activity to fill my time was eating. I found a place on the top floor in the restaurant area where I could look out over the hustle and bustle of the main concourse. I enjoyed a nice perch to watch the constant motion of people below. The restaurant choices were plentiful, as were the food options. They had everything from kimchi and rice to burgers and beer. There were choices of Korean, Chinese, Vietnamese, Japanese, Thai, French, Western cuisine, and, yes, a Starbucks along with Baskin-Robbins Ice Cream. Most prices were reasonable, unlike airport food in the US. It looked like they were trying to satisfy the food preferences of any traveler coming through the airport. I ate mostly from the Korean restaurants, or one of the others featuring Asian food. As in Mongolia, I took a chance ordering some selections with no idea what the ingredients might be. I must say, some meals were better than others.

In the restrooms, I was mildly surprised to see a sign showing people how to use the toilet, instructing them to sit, rather than squatting on top. At first, I thought that was an odd thing. Then I realized that, with missing middle floorboard outhouses so common, toilets may be new to some people.

As the day went on, I enjoyed spending time in front of the giant four-story Jumbotron. The massive screen ran a 40-to-50-minute loop of odd and sometimes bizarre video clips. There were flowers, fireworks displays, poetry, Van Gogh artwork, tigers in the jungle, strange animations, and even liquor ads. Some videos appeared to promote an upcoming art exhibit, but I couldn't read the language. One of my favorites was an adorable clip of puppies and kittens playing together. Nearby, a tropical-themed seating area provided a pleasant view, with benches surrounded by realistic-looking artificial trees. However, the screen was large enough to be seen clearly from any of the four floors facing it.

That night I learned a lesson the hard way - don't wait until midnight to find a place to sleep. There was an area on the lowest level of the airport called "Spa on Air," which offered showers and rooms for sleeping. I was looking forward to renting a room with a soft bed for eight hours of sleep. Unfortunately, I had spent a lot of time wandering around the airport before finally heading to the spa. That was a mistake. By the time I arrived, there was already a long line. I stood there for a while and then realized we were not moving. They may have let a few people in, but I was far enough back that I was not going anywhere. After about 45 minutes, a man came out of the spa holding a "Sorry, Full" sign. A collective groan rippled through the line as people picked up their bags and walked away.

Having already scouted the entire airport, I knew of a few quiet spots that might work for a few hours of sleep. The challenge was finding something comfortable to lie on. I tried a chair first, then a bench. Both were hard and lumpy, but I managed to get a little sleep. The eye mask from my first Ulaanbaatar flight helped block the lights, but it

How to use a toilet

Four-story airport entertainment

could not stop the constant din of background noise throughout the night. Airports like this are 24-hour hubs of activity, with passengers arriving and departing at all hours. The constant low-grade hum of people in motion was just loud enough to keep me from falling into a deep sleep.

As if that wasn't enough, the luggage cart man was busy all night. This poor man, dressed in his white uniform, drove around in a little car collecting empty luggage carts and returning them to a central area. That was fine - except that to alert people of his presence, a computer-generated tone repeated "...be it ever so humble, there's no place like home..." over and over again. It wasn't an entire song, just that one line droning on endlessly. These men drive around day and night without ever changing the tune. They must leave work and still hear it playing in their heads. I was only there for one day, and it nearly drove me insane! I understand the need to alert people, but would it hurt to mix up the music a little bit?

OCTOBER 5: SEOUL TO DALLAS TO HOME

My flight to Dallas was scheduled to leave at 5:40 p.m. I still had an entire day to wander around the airport, which I was beginning to know well. I think airports are great places, but they offer limited things to do. Of course, most people don't spend a full day there, much less all night. The plentiful selection of restaurants kept me happy, since I do like to eat. I also liked to nap, and setting an alarm on my phone allowed me to try and catch up on the sleep I missed the night before without worrying about oversleeping. I would have hated sleeping through the boarding process! Otherwise, there wasn't much to do. Serious boredom began to set in, and time moved slowly. I couldn't even call Val or the kids because daytime in Seoul was nighttime at home.

I made a point to go through the security screening very early to avoid any last-minute issues that might have prevented me from boarding on time. Although the lines were long, there were no other security problems that I encountered. I did everything possible to ensure that when the once-daily flight left, I would be on it. There was no way I was calling Val and telling her I missed my flight because I did something stupid.

After getting through security and finding my departure gate, I found a comfortable seat and watched people go by. There were folks from all over the world speaking all kinds of languages on their way to who knows where. That was the best entertainment I could find. There were several gift shops with last-minute items or magazines for sale, where I bought two small Mongolian flag patches to put on my backpacks. Although I was tired, I didn't dare take another nap. There was no way I would do anything that might make me miss this flight.

Finally, the moment I had been waiting for had arrived. The boarding process began! I boarded the plane and quickly found my seat, a cramped middle seat in economy in the rear of the nearly full 787 for the long flight to Dallas. I could not be happier! The people on each side of me seemed just as tired as I was and not interested in talking. I was OK with that, because I was just happy to be headed home.

With phone, headphones, and eye mask in hand, the carry-on backpack was placed in the overhead compartment, and I kicked off my shoes. My luggage tracker showed the big backpack was on the plane, so I had nothing else to worry about. I really missed my wife, and soon I would see her again. I also missed our dog Ziggy. Val said just after I had left, Ziggy went from room to room at home looking for me. More recently, she told me that he no longer did that, probably thinking I am not coming back. I was really sad to think he could have forgotten me.

Soon the big jet was airborne and turned east over the Pacific Ocean. The window view from the middle seat wasn't that great, so I settled in for dinner and a movie. I don't remember what movie I watched, and it really didn't matter. All I wanted to do was get to Dallas.

Somehow, I managed to sleep a bit as we crossed the ocean and multiple time zones. I would occasionally check the flight path map on the seatback screen, and I smiled when we entered North America. The approach took us over Canada and the western US. We finally arrived in Dallas right on time. I am always amazed when these big planes have such a gentle landing. After we taxied and parked, it took a while for those of us back in economy class to deplane. I was in no rush since I had a long layover with plenty of time to spare.

I quickly zipped through US Customs with my Global Entry card – which was a good investment to speed up the travel experience. The last step in the process was to pick up my checked backpack and have it inspected by the Customs official. Assuring them I did not have farm products, weapons, or other contraband, I then placed the backpack on another conveyor belt to be loaded for the flight home. It was tagged in Seoul to go all the way through to my final destination of Nashville, which made it easy.

I made it to the gate for the flight home in plenty of time. It still seems bizarre to think that when leaving Seoul in the early evening for a 13-hour flight across multiple time zones and the International Date Line, I would arrive in Dallas on the same day in the late afternoon, one hour before my departure time in Seoul. This made for a very long Wednesday!

It was a joyful call to tell Val that I was almost home! We were thankful that my evening flight home was on schedule. This would be my seventh and final flight of the trip. A flight app calculated that all the flights together totaled 18,377 miles. That is about ¾ the circumference of the earth!

The final flight home was full of anticipation. I was grateful to have a window seat. It was evening, and as the sunlight disappeared I could still make out numerous cities and landmarks. The myriads of pinpoint lights signifying civilization below were not seen over the barren land of Mongolia.

As we made the descent to land, I could see the familiar cityscape of home. After landing, the taxiing to the terminal seemed, at least to me, to take an agonizingly long time. Getting off the plane and waiting by the baggage carousel also seemed to take forever. I kept saying to myself "Hurry up! All I needed was one backpack!! Surely it will be the next bag out!" My backpack made it halfway around the world and yes, it made it to that baggage carousel too.

Val and Ziggy were in the Cell Waiting lot. With my backpack in hand, I called Val to come get me. I had been imagining this moment for weeks. Never underestimate the magic of a hug! In the distance I could see a familiar car approaching. As it drove closer, I could see my wonderful wife with a big smile on her face. As the car stopped, Ziggy went ballistic with joy, and I knew he remembered me. Val got out, and that magical moment I had been thinking about for so long finally happened. We hugged each other with tears in our eyes. We held each other long enough so that the airport security guy came over to yell at us to keep moving. We didn't care. This was our moment.

Val, Ziggy, and I home again

About the Author

Dr. John VanOstenbridge lives with his wife, Val, outside Nashville, Tennessee, with their dog, Ziggy. John is a retired pediatrician with an adventurous spirit who enjoys hiking, biking, kayaking, and outdoor fun. Eager to find the travel adventure of a lifetime, John said yes to a bizarre invitation and found a new world of culture, climate, and challenge that he will never forget.